Bridge the Gap
How One Church
Partnered with a
Public School

Brian Stroh

To Tarina, Riley, Wesley, Charley, and Kinsley-

Thank you for your grace and loving support during this project and living out what it means to bridge the gap

CONTENTS

BRIAN STROH

Praise for *Bridge the Gap*

Brian Stroh has provided an excellent resource that helps churches, ministries and followers of Christ know how to impact their local schools in both needed, and meaningful ways. I encourage all pastors and leaders to read this book while asking the question, "How does God want to use US to benefit the students, teachers, administration and families in OUR neighborhood?" - and then be ready to answer that question with action! *Tom Henderson, Author, Speaker and Founder of Restoration Generation*

Bridge the Gap is an informational and inspirational guide that provides practical tools on how to share the love of Christ through partnering with local schools to make a lasting impact. This is a must read for all faith leaders and influencers ready to reach their community for Christ. *Trevor Hislop, Pastor of Service Programming, Church at Viera*

Pastor Brian has been instrumental in Bridge(ing) the Gap in his own community for the past decade and now he both invites and challenges us to do the same. Readers will be blessed by Stroh's honesty, humor and stories from the trenches. A generous and sacrificial example of loving God by loving others, this is a must read for Christians. *Myra Katherine Hale, Author and Speaker*

As a principal that was fortunate to be on the receiving end of many of the actions and gifts given to (Cleveland) our school, I can tell you first-hand what an impact every gesture made. Our school never felt like our business partnership was about growing Sunday morning attendance but always knew it was about Christ's love in unselfish contributions. In the book, you will have a hint of Brian's humor and his wit which only adds to the ease of reading this "hey, we've done this and you can too" guide. *Jackie McNamara, former Cleveland Principal, South Dakota Principal of the Year*

Prologue

What are you going to do on your sabbatical?

This book is the answer to that question.

That question kept coming.

It came from family members.

It came from friends.

It came from those I served at Hillcrest, who certainly had—or have—a vested interest in how I am going to be spending my extended time away from them and my work responsibilities.

When I first started thinking about this sabbatical, writing a book was not the answer I was giving to the obvious question that had yet to come. My plan looked more 'sabbatically'—probably made up a word there—and included time for renewal, reflection, and reading. But as the 'what are you going to do' question kept coming, I discovered that I did in fact want to do something. I wanted to have some proof that this sabbatical was not just a once in a lifetime June, July, and August—an extended summer vacation—that few people ever get once they leave school. I want to be able to look back after three months and say, "This. This is what I did while I was away."

It is possible that there is some pride involved—it is always possible that there is some pride involved—but the older I get, and the quicker 40 comes at me, the more I realize that I am a doer. I get things done. When people ask another of those obvious questions—"So, what do you do?"—the answer I want to say is that "I get things done." It would seem rather disingenuous, then, to come to the realization that 'someone who gets things done' takes a three-month break and doesn't get anything done.

As soon as I told Tarina and a few folks about the idea for this book, the whole concept was challenged within the week before I was to begin the sabbatical and write the book.

It was a Friday. Tarina and I were off from work and at home when we got a call from Cleveland, the school where our youngest two children attend and the subject for most of what follows. There had been an incident at the playground. A boy in our daughter's class had shown Kinsley a pocket knife that he had brought to school during morning recess. The boy also threatened Kinsley by saying he'd throw the knife at her if she told anyone. Kinsley knew better. She went to find a teacher while the boy ran away. Kinsley met with the assistant principal, who affirmed her decision, and she was sent back to class. The couple hours between the phone call and picking up Kinsley from school were a whirlwind of 'what if' scenarios:

- What if the boy isn't punished or expelled?
- What if Kinsley is really upset about this incident?
- What if the boy is allowed to return to the school next year?
- What if the other kids in the classroom tease Kinsley for being a snitch?
- What if Kinsley wants to change schools but Charley, our youngest son, who would only have one more year at the school, doesn't?
- What if, what if, what if?

As a person of faith, I do not really believe in coincidence or accident. I found it somewhat comical—and challenging—that the week I was revealing what my sabbatical book project was going to be about was also the same time this serious incident occurred.

Doubt crept in.

Anxiety began to take over.

How could I write a book on a school where I wasn't even sure it was the best place for my daughter at this moment in time?

How could I tell the story of all the good that had occurred at Cleveland and Hillcrest while simultaneously having discussions on whether this was the right school, at this time, for our kids?

How could I advocate that families and followers of Jesus send their children to their local neighborhood schools when I was questioning if we were going to be sending ours to that local neighborhood school?

I mean there's hypocrisy, and then there's *this* hypocrisy!

At the time of writing, the situation involving Kinsley and the boy with the knife had calmed down.

The most important factor was Kinsley was good. She felt proud for making the right decision, and there did not seem to be any residual effect from friends, classmates, or teachers.

The next most important factor was that the boy was removed from school for the remainder of the school year. I admit that sounds like a rather odd 'next most important factor' for an author to share in a book about all the good (and the messiness) that occurs when people of faith seek to serve their local schools.

I want to see this boy redeemed.

I want to see this boy make positive decisions.

I want to see this boy know his worth and value as a person and that he too has a future that he can write.

Yet there are consequences for poor decisions. Bringing a knife to school is one such example of a poor decision. And in this situation, the final poor decision in a year of poor decisions. Seeking to do good in an under-resourced school doesn't mean having to ignore other realities. Seeking to do good doesn't mean ignoring that a student brought a weapon to school.

This incident certainly tested our family's mettle, our commitment, our belief in what we were doing when it came to the intersection of our faith and our children's education.

The pages that follow tell a story of a normal church—made up of normal people, normal leadership, and a normal budget—who undertook an endeavor to serve a normal school that ended up radically affecting both the church and the school.

Chapter 1: The Neighborhood School No One in the Neighborhood Went to

As a Cleveland employee, I am deeply touched by the love, support, gifts, and time Hillcrest folks have given to us. Never have I had a business partner with a school that was so invested in the kids, teachers, and well-being of all who walk through our doors. Your kindness has gone far beyond what I would expect. Your loyalty to our school/school needs is priceless.

Emily Lafrentz, Cleveland first-grade teacher

How come none of the kids in the neighborhood go to the neighborhood school?

It was an innocent enough question I asked 'to the trees,' a phrase Tarina and I use when we ask questions that we don't really know the answer to and know that the other also doesn't have an answer to. It's also the kind of question that Google can't answer. I mean, you can type those words into Google, and you'll get answers—the top current result is a Washington, DC, mom blogger.

Ten years ago, our oldest son, Riley, was preparing to head to school. Our home was a half-mile from Cleveland Elementary School, the neighborhood school within our district. Cleveland was the school he—and every other kid that played at our house—was supposed to attend. Yet in a neighborhood of 15 school-aged children—no one from our half of the block attended the school only half a mile away from our homes!

The question I asked the trees was why?

Why did two families homeschool their children rather than send them to the school a half-mile away?

Why did two other families send their children to two different private schools rather than send them to the school a half-mile away?

Why did another two families open-enroll their children to a different public school rather than send them to the school a half-mile away?

Why, in a neighborhood that had 15 school-aged children—not counting our four that would soon be school-aged—living in six different homes—did none attend the neighborhood school?

The school a half-mile away.

The school in our district.

The school that all our kids would have attended if these other decisions weren't made.

How come none of the kids in the neighborhood go to the neighborhood school?

Education Is Like Sex—No One Wants to Talk About It

I grew up going to the neighborhood school. My siblings and I attended the school in the district where we lived along with every other kid in the neighborhood. Going to school in the 1980s, the only other option was parochial schools. Open enrollment and charter schools hadn't been invented yet. And no one dared homeschool their kids—who did that?

Attending a neighborhood school meant going to school with your buddies. We played on the same basketball teams as the kids we went to school with. We played on the same baseball teams as the kids we went to school with. We played hot box, street hockey, deer hunter, and a host of other games that we made up with the rest of the neighborhood kids that we went to school with. While there certainly may have been the rare kid or two who did not attend the neighborhood school (most likely that kid went to a parochial school), most of us neighborhood kids went to the same school.

Obviously, times and culture have changed since I attended school. Families have a multitude of options when it comes to their child's education.

Private schools.

Charter schools.

Open-enrolling students to a different, better, higher performing school.

Homeschooling.

Online schooling.

Some families further customize their family's experience with education, with one child at a private school and another child at a public school.

Education is quickly becoming a "to each their own" topic we treat with the same societal taboo as politics, sex, money, and religion. A topic where we seek out like-minded folks who have made the same decision as we have made and can commiserate with one another. A topic where if we find out a family or friend has made a decision different then our own, we say something along the lines of "oh, that's great" but privately judge them for their decisions and question our own.

As further evidence between the thin line of asking these questions and being a hypocrite, when we were first deciding on where to send Riley to school, he was attending kindergarten at the private school where Tarina taught preschool!

Yes, we were asking a question of why no kids went to the local school when we opted our oldest son out of kindergarten at that school! Go ahead, say it.

Hypocrite!

Riley received the benefit of a half-day kindergarten classroom steps away from where Tarina taught. On his first day, Tarina is teary-eyed, of course, and the tears are compounded by kindergarten drop-off stories she heard on the radio on her way to work. She is trying to hold it together to ready her own class for preschool students who would arrive the following week when her administrative assistant comforts her and asks where Riley is going to kindergarten.

Tarina replies, "Down the hall. In our kindergarten class."

The administrative assistant, instantly feeling less compassion, replies, "Oh, well then get it together!"

We knew we couldn't swing that decision for the rest of the kids—even with the discount, it was still expensive (or an investment, depending on your perspective). Besides, her school didn't offer anything beyond kindergarten, so the thought of private school beyond kindergarten was not an option for us. Our intention was always to have our kids in public school.

In the World but Not of It

Tarina and I both possess the same "in the world but not of the world" mentality. Those words come to us loosely from one of Jesus' last recorded prayers in John 17, when he prays in verse 15, "I'm not asking you to take them out of the world, but to keep them safe from the evil one," and also later in verse 18 when he prays, "I am sending them into the world." In the Christian circles I am most accustomed to, these verses provide the foundation for the perspective of "in the world, but not of the world." It's the mantra Christians use to stay connected to culture but not become part of it.

The whole context behind this prayer is one of sanctification, but not sanctification in the terms Christians usually think of. Most of the time when Christians hear sanctify or sanctification, we think of holiness. We think of separation. We think of putting things into categories like Christian and non-Christian, sacred and secular. Yet the deeper one dives into this prayer by Jesus, the more one discovers that Jesus' prayer is one of action and involvement, not one of one passivity and separation. Jesus never intends for his disciples to establish a way of life that is separate from others within the world. He doesn't expect his disciples to pull back, establish a monastery or commune where they reflect on their time with Jesus and his amazing teaching, and yet never do anything.

It's why the Great Commission is a challenge with actions—go, make, baptize.

It's why in Acts 1 Jesus' last words to his disciples talk about being witnesses in Jerusalem, Judea, Samaria, and the ends of the earth.

It's why, when you get to the end of Acts, the believers took his words seriously and lived them out, and why the gospel at that point had spread in all four cardinal directions. The known world—at that time – had heard about Jesus because the disciples lived out John 17. They were in the world but committed to not being of it.

Halloween and Public School

One of the first messages I preached at Hillcrest was on this very passage titled "Halloween: Good or Bad?"

The message was received about as well as you could imagine.

I am by no means a great teacher or preacher today, but I was much less so back then. I violated my preaching professor's cardinal rule of preaching, which was never use a text to support an argument you already have!

Back to the Halloween sermon. Ten years ago, churches were doing some pretty weird things to not get too involved with Halloween. They were putting on harvest parties or fall festivals around the time of Halloween. While the event was called a party or festival, these events eerily resembled a Halloween party, though so long as the word "Harvest" was in it, it was all good. Because so many in my suburban church context had a deep connection to harvest time, and it had to be recognized!

Whether a harvest festival or party, the elements were all there.

First, children dressed in costume. The more progressive churches only disallowed scary or inappropriate costumes—meaning Spider Man was okay. More traditional churches requested kids dress up as their favorite Bible character, so Spider Man was out, but Samson is in.

Second, games were played. There would be hay bales for photos, containers with apples for bobbing, and a jump house or some other inflatable.

Finally, candy would be given out. The goal was to make the event 'worth it' for the Christian kid, so said Harvest Festival, if done right, would make sure the kid got a TON of candy. Some of it was earned by the playing of carnival-like games, while some was merely received by going from station to station and simply getting candy for being in a costume. Novel. Wonder where that idea came from?

I'm not sure whom we thought we were kidding, but we were having a Halloween party and calling it a Harvest Party. Finally, the inevitable happened, and the Harvest Party landed on a Wednesday night. How great! It was ideal! Our kids wouldn't miss out on trick or treating because they'd get to do it at the church's Harvest Party!

From a John 17 perspective, though, it was a miss. We took families out of their neighborhoods, their communities, their worlds and brought them into an alternative world where the kids got to do the same thing, except it wasn't Halloween. Ed Stetzer, author and Christian researcher, says it best: "You don't have to worship the devil to go up and ask your neighbor for candy."

So, I gave a message. I dissected Jesus' words in John 17. I argued that his words were the perfect words for how a Christian and a church should answer the Halloween question. I did admit that there are many traditions and imagery associated with Halloween that do not honor God, but I also argued that had Halloween existed in first century Palestine, I do not believe that Jesus and his disciples would have hunkered in for the night and not left their porch-candle on, begging for first century Jewish boys and girls to egg their houses for their lack of generosity! I argued in the message that Christians have a responsibility to engage with Halloween, connect with neighbors, and yes, give out candy! Some agreed. Many did not. It was an early lesson not only in the messiness of ministry—over 200 people would leave our church in the upcoming months (not because of that message, but certainly because of the philosophical change that and other messages were communicating)—but it was also an early lesson in the messiness of seeking to live a life that is in the world, but not of the world.

These words of Jesus from John 17 are so important that they comprise one of our family's five values: presence. Yeah, we're one of those nerd families that has identified some core values and tries—tries—to live them out. We include the motto "in the world, but not of the world" with this value of presence. It guides our family's decisions, from education, to extra-curricular activities, to how we spend our free time. We had decided to live out our value of presence by sending our kids to the local school no one else was sending their kids to, and we would soon discover why our neighbors were not sending theirs.

Chapter 2: Not My Kid

I have enjoyed working with Hillcrest because they are willing to help and go above and beyond, they truly understand our students/population.

Gretchen Johnson, Cleveland's physical education teacher and former Sioux Falls' Teacher of the Year

Psychologists tell us that a person's perception is their reality.

There are also moments when the perception *is* the reality.

Tarina and I never conducted sit-down interviews with our neighbors as to why only one kid went to Cleveland, but we got the sense that Cleveland was a 'less-than' school.

A school that didn't do as well as other schools with standardized testing.

A school that had more diversity than other schools.

A school with greater economic challenges then other schools.

The presence of these factors seemed to be driving our neighbors' decisions about their children's education. The educational statistics backed up their perceptions. In 2007—as it is now—Cleveland was a Title I School, meaning its scores are lower than the federal guidelines.

In 2007,

- 20% of Cleveland's students had a diagnosed disability, the sixth-highest such percentage of Sioux Falls' public schools

- 20% of Cleveland's students were classified as ESL (English as a Second Language), the second-highest such percentage of Sioux Falls' public schools
- 48% of Cleveland's students were either on free or reduced meal plans.

In 2015, eight years later, the perception and reality still exist. In December 2015, the *Argus Leader* (the local newspaper) ran an article titled: "Open enrollment: Schools a mile apart on different ends of debate." The article highlighted my original question with the discovery that over 40 students open-enrolled from Cleveland to Harvey Dunn Elementary. Among the reasons the article cited as to why families open-enroll students from neighborhood school to a different school: test scores and less diversity. The article also revealed that in 2015 72% of Cleveland's students qualified for free or reduced meal plans, while 33% of Cleveland's students were classified as ESL students.

Christians Pulling Out of Public School

The overall perception of public education is not that good. This rather small example of families pulling students from a lower performing school to a higher performing school is probably not all that new. What is newer, though, is the growing trend or belief that Christians ought not to attend any public school. Matt Walsh, the Christian columnist and political incendiary, outlines the argument for Christians to pull their kids from public school in the article titled "Christian Parents, your kids aren't equipped to be public school missionaries." His article describes the perceived increasing hostility of the public school system to Christians and that many Christian students and families are ill-equipped to navigate—much less thrive or even challenge (for the better)—such an environment.

The numbers back up Walsh's claim, at least in terms of the popularity of home-schooling:

- The number of home-schooled children increased in the United States by 61.8 percent from 2003-2012.
- Home-school enrollment has risen 40% in South Dakota since 2010.
- The number of homeschoolers in Sioux Falls has nearly doubled since 2009.

One of the more popular narratives within my Christian subculture aligns with Walsh's argument. Christian families are indeed looking at a public school system that is increasingly hostile toward their values and beliefs and are choosing instead to educate their own children in a much more controlled environment that better matches their beliefs and values.

Home-schooling and other educational options are not just for Christians, however. In 2011, the marketing guru and best-selling author Seth Godin made the reading recommendation of *Weapons of Mass Instruction: A Schoolteacher's Journey Through the Dark World of Compulsory Schooling* by John Taylor Gatto. I am big fan of Seth's work and also whatever he recommends, so I read the book. It's an interesting and at times disturbing read. Gatto essentially argues that the contemporary public school system is set up as a holdover from Prussia, and more recently, 20th-century Germany, where school is a massive organizational tool to control children and train them to be employees for large corporations (a hallmark for the 20th century). The system is also designed to mold students into consumers of the products made by those same corporations. Gatto believes that people who succeed in school are merely training to succeed in the system of corporate rule following and mindless consumption. He argues that as modern schooling has advanced, our literacy rate and other key benchmarks for learning have actually decreased. The public school system certainly has the potential to condition students—and especially boys—to follow rules, to take turns, to not talk out of turn, to sit in desks without being squirrely, to treat active elements such as physical education and the natural world as extracurriculars (and thus outsourced to organizations like the Scouts, youth sports leagues, and the Y), where precious little time is given while they are in school.

It's a difficult book and argument because I think that public educators have some of the toughest jobs on the planet. When I go to school, I can't imagine the tenacity and perseverance it takes to try and teach day in and day out. I understand feeling disillusioned. I understand feeling frustrated. I get feeling that with increasing standards and test scores and AYP (adequate yearly progress) and federal standards and increasing behavior issues, how difficult it must be to actually teach reading or math or science.

And yet, if every Christian family, if all Christian parents pull their kids from the public school system, are we not admitting failure?

Are we not just giving up?

Are we not just abdicating a critical part of our culture and shrugging our shoulders and saying "oh well" to those without the option or mobility to make such a decision?

If Christians abandon the public school system, who will be there to make a difference?

Not My Kid

You've heard of NIMBY—Not In My Back Yard. We use this term to describe any development that we're typically for—a manufacturing plant, a new retail center, a non-profit that resources felons leaving prison—so long as it's not in our backyard. We like the program, the development, the progress, so long as it's somewhere else. Not in our neighborhood.

Perhaps a new acronym when it comes to partnering with the local school is NMK—Not My Kid.

In the following chapters we'll walk through some things we did at Hillcrest to come alongside and be a business partner for Cleveland Elementary. We'll highlight things that went well and things that we learned from. And while we've been Cleveland's business partner for several years now and Hillcresters are tremendously proud of the work we do alongside the teachers and staff, the perception still exists that it's a school many families might think twice before sending their own kids to. I would extend this argument even further and say that while many of us are excited at the potential of a church-school partnership and the ministry opportunities, those same folks still make very different and optimal education choices for our own children. We may like that our church is partnering with an under-resourced or challenging school, but we would never consider sending our own children to that same school. We reason that it wouldn't be in our own children's best interests to make such a decision.

The few books that I've read on church-school partnership seem to illustrate this point. Authors of book such as *The Jonathan Effect* and *Real Hope in Chicago* detail fantastic ministry within local schools and neighborhoods much more challenging and with greater results then Hillcrest's work with Cleveland. And yet both authors were able to make different educational decisions than the communities they were serving. Both of them were able to send children to private schools while serving a demographic that could never send children to private schools.

I've worked alongside local pastors who set out with their children in the disadvantaged neighborhood school only to end up open-enrolling their children to 'better' schools after a couple of years.

These statements sound judgmental, but they demonstrate the greatest challenge with this kind of ministry. As much as we can do and partner with under-resourced schools and neighborhoods, there's the reality that the people doing the ministry have more options and choices when it comes to their own economic and educational choices.

Call it reality.

Call it privilege.

Call it whatever you want.

It's interesting to witness middle- and upper-class people doing ministry in a poorer context and then be able to retreat to different neighborhoods, different districts, and live a much different life.

The day I wrote this particular rant I ran into an acquaintance I hadn't seen in quite some time. After exchanging pleasantries, we talked for a few minutes about the need for schools—districts really—to resist segregating along socioeconomic lines. The acquaintance remarked about her school's closing and merging with a different school. Her school had a poorer demographic and was merging with a school with a much more upper middle-class population. There was resistance from the existing, richer school from taking in the students from the poorer school. While the merger went through fine, this teacher revealed the types of discussions—and fear—that occur in our community and most likely through communities throughout our nation.

Robert Putnam, in his book *Our Kids: The American Dream in Crisis*, lays out a strong argument for more involvement in local schools, especially those under-resourced schools:

- *"The presence in a classroom of kids who had been exposed to domestic violence reduced other kids' achievement, especially in high-poverty schools."* This in part explains my neighbors' decision to seek education outside of the local school. The under-resourced students brought trauma, through no fault of their own, into the classroom on a daily basis. This trauma not only impacted their learning but has residual effects on the rest of the classroom's ability to learn.

- *"Even if we harden our hearts and simply leave these poor kids to fend for themselves, we still have to reckon with the lion's share of these costs."* Many well-intentioned families seek to avoid this type of learning environment to do better for their own children. While there's certainly nothing immoral or wrong about such a choice, if everyone makes that same choice, not only do we end up with school for 'haves' and schools for 'have nots,' we also only delay the eventual cost—both financial and moral—that such a decision will have on a community. Mike Tenbusch, author of the *The Jonathan Effect*, argues America's most troubled and failing high schools end up being pipelines to America's prisons, whose existence are funded by taxpayers. It only makes civic sense and financial prudence to consider pouring resources into the front end of an under-resourced child's education rather than making cuts there only to have to pick up the tab later.

- *"Many teachers in poor schools today are doing a heroic job, driven by idealism, but in a market economy the most obvious way to attract more and better teachers to such demanding work is to improve the conditions of their employment."* Until 2016, South Dakota ranked dead last in teacher compensation. Complicating the matter was that teachers in states that bordered South Dakota—mainly North Dakota, Minnesota, Iowa, and Nebraska—made about $6,000–$8,000 more than South Dakota's teachers. Teacher pay is always a hot topic. It affects taxes and raises questions of appropriate spending. While there are merits to the discussion, Putnam's point remains that teachers with market skills will and do leave schools to pursue other endeavors and greater pay. We can argue against it, challenge it, and say "it ain't so," but if we want our brightest to educate the next generation, we need to make it worth it for them to do so.

Business leaders are also taking notice at the opportunities present with partnering with a public school. Marc Benioff, the CEO of Salesforce, had this to say in Tim Ferris' book *Tribe of Mentors*:

> Nothing is more important than our children's education. If kids don't have a K-12 education, they won't have a chance in the future, especially for jobs that require competencies in core subjects like mathematics and writing. I've adopted my local school, Presidio Middle School, in San Francisco. It was fortuitous that I adopted the school my mother went to, even though I didn't know it at the time. It was like I was directed there in some strange way.
>
> By adopting a school, we can do relatively small amounts of work that have a huge and lasting impact. Today, schools are often isolated from their communities, including local businesses. Making a difference is as simple as knocking on the door of your neighborhood school and asking the principal how you can help. You'd be surprised by how this simple act can change the lives of young students for the better. It's great to focus on parochial schools, charter schools, and other schools, but they are not the vast majority of school in the United States. The 3.5 million public school teachers in the US, who make an average of $38,000 a year, need our help and our support to prepare our children for the future. They're only going to get that if every one of us pitches in and adopts a school.

(p. 449)

Those with the means and the opportunity have the freedom to make those kinds of decisions. They can open-enroll to another school. They can sell their home and buy a home in a preferred district. One of our old neighbors did just that, buying a house less than half a mile from their existing house, simply to attend a perceived better school without the annual hassle of open enrollment forms. They can opt for private school or even homeschooling. The point is not that these options are without sacrifice—of course they are. The point is that so many of the families who attend Cleveland and other similar schools do not have the freedom to even consider these choices. Their children's futures are impacted by the overall school and its performance.

In *Hillbilly Elegy,* J.D. Vance writes:

> We don't need to live like the elites of California, New York, or Washington D.C. We don't need to work a hundred hours at law firms and investment banks. We don't need to socialize at cocktail parties. We do need to create a space for the JDs and Brians of the world to have a chance. I don't know what the answer is, precisely, but I know it starts when we stop blaming Obama or Bush or faceless companies and ask ourselves what we can do to make things better.

(p. 256)

Earlier, he writes about questions most of us face when leaning in and coming alongside under-resourced people in an attempt to make things better:

> How much of our lives, good and bad, should we credit to our personal decisions, and how much is just the inheritance of our culture, our families, and our parents who have failed their children? How much is Mom's life her own fault? Where does blame stop and sympathy begin?

(p. 231)

Are the problems that Putnam and Vance write about our problem—my problem—or someone else's?

Chapter 3: Preparing for Partnership

This has stretched me in that I can't parent my mentee but need to be his friend. It is a work in progress. Jesus has a real soft spot in his heart for kids, and I think it honors him for us to model that.

Darwin Gramstad, nurse anesthetist and former chairman of Hillcrest's Leadership Council

At the same time Tarina and I were asking questions about our neighborhood school, Hillcrest was also asking some very foundational questions. The questions stemmed from the book *The Church of Irresistible Influence: Bridge-Building Stories to Help Reach Your Community* by Robert Lewis. Lewis pastored a church in Little Rock, AK, that had remarkable success with their efforts at serving their community. In May 2007, they hosted a conference Pastor Doug and I would attend and further be confronted with two questions that would fundamentally change how we approach ministry and how Hillcrest operates as a church:

- Are the people in my life better off because of my relationship with Jesus?
- Would anyone protest if Hillcrest were to cease to exist as a church?

The first question is why Tarina and I would intentionally send our children to Cleveland.

The second question would launch our church's partnership with Cleveland, because an honest answer to the second question would be "no."

Our neighbors—those who physically lived in close proximity to us—would not miss us. Outside of our annual summer block party, we didn't do much for them or with them. They tolerated us, tolerated our summer block party and youth ministry kegger event (that's a good story, too!), but we weren't doing much for them. We weren't providing much value for them. There wasn't anything great about living next door to a church.

Our city would not miss us. We weren't doing anything for them. While we supported some local non-profits with minimal financial assistance, we weren't actively serving these organizations, and the ones we did occasionally serve with were mainly places already serving other Christians.

Our world would not miss us. The handful of global missionaries we were supporting at the time would miss our financial contributions, but we rarely heard from them. They didn't visit us on furlough, and we didn't really seem to care if they visited us or not. Foreign missions was a check we wrote—similar to your utility bill. You pay the water bill, you get the benefit of water, but you really don't consider the greatness of what water is and what it brings to your life. Same with missions. As long as we kept writing checks to our global missionaries, we got the benefit of saying we supported global missions, but we really didn't consider the greatness of what missions is and what it could bring to the life of a church. We were not necessary to these missionaries' success on the field. We did it because that is something a good church did.

It had also been decades since a Hillcrester had been called to missions. And how could one? When the priority for missions is merely a financial one treated like a monthly bill and nothing more, we were not doing much to highlight the possibility for Hillcresters of what the Great Commission might look like in our world.

As we wrestled with how we would answer the question of would anyone protest if Hillcrest ceased to exist as a church, one thing became clear—no matter how we answered that question, we had to do better with our missions funding and missions initiatives. It is common for churches to simply add on programs, missionaries, or causes without ever considering why a church is supporting a cause or a mission organization. One of our attenders was passionate about a rodeo Bible camp, so we supported that. Another was passionate about prison ministry, so we supported that. We had no idea how these fit within our overall purpose or strategy but knew we didn't like saying "no" to mission requests. We soon found ourselves with an outreach budget supporting over 25 different missionaries and mission organizations, but without really knowing what any of these missionaries or mission organizations actually did and never serving alongside them or with them.

Missions Audit

It was time for a missions audit. We knew if we were going to be the type of church that the community would miss, we would have to get serious about our existing partnerships or stop those partnerships in order to begin new ones. There's lots of books out there on best practices when it comes to leading a church or an organization through change. We landed on the concept of a missions audit, where we would gauge how connected our church was to the various missions organizations we were supporting and see if there might be space to make some changes. That summer we were without an outreach elder, so I was leading that team in the interim time. Our missions audit looked like this: we designed a 20-question, multiple-choice quiz to see how well our outreach team knew the missionaries and organizations that we supported.

The questions were rather simple.

What does Organization A do?

Where does Missionary Y serve?

Who is the executive director of Camp Z, where our students attend every summer?

Twenty multiple-choice questions given to the people who decide our missions priorities and determine their funding from our operational budget.

The results?

The highest score was an 8.

The average score was a 4.

These were from the outreach team. If our outreach team did not know who these people were and what these places did, how could we expect other Hillcresters to know?

We began the necessary but difficult work of making sure we knew where our missions funds went. That we knew the stories behind the line items. That we could take a similar quiz in the future and get a perfect score. That the places and people we supported would be compelled to stop and visit and update Hillcrest because that was how important we were to their mission, because their mission was our mission. We made tough decisions. We stopped supporting several foreign missionaries through our denomination because we had no idea what they did.

These were not easy decisions. The few folks who were passionate about a non-profit or a cause were hurt and disappointed. The foreign missionaries we were supporting were disappointed and confused. Our denomination was mad and upset. I can still recall the rather harsh letter we received from our denomination questioning these decisions and imploring us to reconsider, saying if that we didn't, we'd be failing the missional imperatives outlined in Acts 1:8. Ouch. We knew we were bumping up against something if our denomination was willing to wade into the waters of spiritual manipulation in order to keep our mission funds.

In my 15 years of pastoral ministry in a local church, changes within a church often go through this process of death and rebirth. We had to kill some things that were not consistent with where we were headed as a church. We had to admit that those things we were currently supporting were not helping us become the church the community would miss. We had to stop doing some things so we could be prepared and open to what God was calling us to.

With significant funds now freed up in our mission budget, we pooled some of those funds into greater support of a foreign missionary that we did know—a medical doctor to the African country of Cameroon who was training Cameroonian doctors. We also took some of those now available funds and were able to fully support Hillcrest's first missionary in forever—Jessi Matson (now Jessi Matson Copeland)—who would be serving with an organization called City Mission Academy in inner-city Detroit. Jessi was born at Hillcrest and was following God's call on her life to teach under-resourced children in one of American's worst neighborhoods.

How Can You Help Us?

We also had resources—and just as important, thinking—available to consider what a partnership with a school might look like. The historical relationship between a school and a church often usually falls into one of the following two categories:

- Non-existent—the first category is that sadly, the relationship between a school and a church is non-existent. Neither the school nor the church has considered how their organization could help out the other.
- Mission field—the second category helps explain the first. Churches at times have viewed the local school as a mission field, and thus see it as a way to communicate the gospel and also bring people to their church. I am certainly pro-gospel, but the execution of this plan is often messy and leaves little to be desired from the school's perspective.

The mission field church-school model looks something like this: Church A wants to host an after-school Bible club in School B. The club isn't school-sanctioned due to church-state separation, but School B agrees and allows space to meet. The relationship starts off well enough. School B is friendly and accommodating; leadership from Church A is respectful and considerate. The relationship sours when Church A begins to proselytize and take advantage of the relationship by inviting students to off-campus youth ministry events or asking the school to send home religious materials. The action is classic bait-and-switch theology connected to church growth or conversion statistics. Church A can point to the Bible club as tangible proof of community outreach and then lean on the Bible club to bolster numbers and attendance to its church. School B may initially OK Church A's request, but they are just one complaint or lawsuit away from not being able to. Most leaders within School B already know this and politely usher Church A from being able to host the after-school Bible club. Church A is disappointed but can now use this example as persecution and not being welcomed by the public school.

Those reading this book know that the above story is far from fictional.

Church A uses the school for students and space but fails to consider how they could serve School B's students, teachers, and community. Over time School B grows weary of the relationship, fears it is getting too close to church-state separation matters, and notes that the next time they're presented with such a request, they will for sure pass on it. Church A is then mad and offended, talks about freedom of speech being violated, and considers the treatment they receive from School B as proof of their suffering for the sake of the gospel.

Perhaps there was a third way.

A way where a church built a relationship with a school based on how it could best assist the school without any strings attached.

A way where a church could approach a school with a "how can we help" mindset rather than a "what can you do for us" mindset.

BRIAN STROH

Chapter 4: A Third Way

I read with two classes a year, mostly kindergarten and first grade. Loved it! Appreciated how much the kids craved and responded to individual attention shown them. Most of the kids smiled ear to ear when they were able to come read on a one-on-one basis. They shared not only their reading skills, but their happies, their concerns, their sads. Just having one more adult in their life that was interested in them seemed to be a thrill for them.

Deanna Moser, reading buddy for several classes at Cleveland

Pastor Doug and I had heard the stories. Stories about churches partnering with public schools.

We had heard about them at conferences.

We had read about them in books.

We hadn't seen any examples in Sioux Falls of anyone doing this kind of ministry.

Tarina and I were still wrestling with the neighborhood question of why no one attended Cleveland.

Our church was wrestling with the 'missing you' question.

It was starting to look like Cleveland may be a good fit for both these questions, but some additional background work was required.

One of the first things we did was to see where Hillcresters lived and then identify the elementary school for that address. I love data and what data can tell me. We had a hunch that while our church attracted people from all over the area, many of our families lived close by and sent their kids to schools close by.

The data took some time to crunch, but was no harder than taking a family's address and then inputting it into our district's website, where it spit out the corresponding local elementary school. The results were as follows:

- Hillcresters live in 24 different elementary school districts.
- Of the 24 different elementary school districts, the highest percentage of Hillcresters live in three elementary districts that were closest geographically to our facility:
- 8% of Hillcresters live within the Harvey Dunn district
- 14% of Hillcresters live within the John Harris district
- 15% of Hillcresters live within the Cleveland district.

Cleveland is the second closest school to Hillcrest; Harvey Dunn is the closest. The school with the most Hillcrest families is also one of the schools closest geographically to Hillcrest. It also had much more need than either John Harris or Harvey Dunn, both excellent schools who serve a different socioeconomic demographic than Cleveland.

Armed with our family's question, our church's question, and this data, I had enough information to request a meeting with Cleveland's principal. I outlined the purpose of my requested meeting and made sure to communicate that Hillcrest was not looking to set up an after-school Bible club or looking to run Hillcrest propaganda through her school (the mission field model). We were simply interested in seeing if there were any needs we as a church could help meet, and if so, what that might look like.

Reading Buddies

The first area for need was to be a reading buddy. If you've had kids in school, you know the weekly or monthly reading logs that come home.

Read for 20 minutes a day with your child.

Record every book that your child reads during this month.

This isn't mere busywork. There are several good studies that confirm, among other things, that students who scored 90% or better than their peers on reading tests read for more than 20 minutes a day and are exposed to 1.8 million words a year! That's compared to students who scored at the 50th percentile, who read on average 5 minutes per day and are exposed to 282,000 words a year. The challenge in under-resourced schools is often students are not reading when they are home. With each passing year, these students fall further and further back in reading proficiency and vocabulary mastery, making mastery of other subjects and topics much more difficult. If a student cannot read well, it's going to make biology much more difficult. It's going to make understanding the Civil War much more difficult. It's going to make programming much more difficult. Cleveland needed Hillcresters to come to the school and serve as a reading buddy, someone who listens to students read. They would help these students get the additional practice and time on reading during the school day.

Mentoring

Mentoring—there's lots of research about the benefit of mentoring, but in an under-resourced school environment, there's often a lack of mentors coming alongside children who would most benefit from a mentor. Books such as Mike Tenbusch's *The Jonathan Effect* and Ruby Payne's *Framework for Understanding Poverty* detail the positive effects of adults coming alongside of and mentoring an under-resourced child. Cleveland had no such program in place and saw opportunities for its students to benefit from a caring adult taking an interest in a child and meeting weekly for lunch, playing games, and sharing life together.

Mentoring is one of the initiatives that often gets highlighted as a program that can assist students and adults. Vance, Ruby Payne, and others argue people can only jump up a socioeconomic class if they have a mentor from the class they're trying to reach. The school-based mentoring program we were going to partner with is one such program aiming to give students that kind of opportunity.

The potential for involvement was endless, and there wasn't any other business or church that decided to partner with Cleveland. This was important for Hillcrest, as we didn't want to steal someone's else thunder, but it also affirmed that we were looking at the right place to build a potential bridge into the community.

Our great conversation concluded with learning that the lead principal I had just met with was being sent to another school, and the assistant principal would be splitting time the upcoming school year between Cleveland and a different school.

Things that could have been brought to my attention yesterday!

A potential roadblock meant another meeting, with a new principal, and the uncertainty of whether the new principal would be as open as the one I had just met with.

Homework

In the months between my first meeting with Cleveland and meeting with the new principal, we had additional homework to complete.

We conducted a good ol'-fashioned SWOT analysis where we identified Hillcrest's Strengths, Weaknesses, Opportunities, and Threats when it came to what a partnership could look like.

We polled our congregation for ways Hillcrest could better answer the 'would anyone miss us' question and discovered our people had a heart for children and assisting under-resourced children.

We discovered that several Hillcresters had backgrounds in education or were already employed as teachers and thus would be instrumental in our initial planning and discussions.

We drafted a plan for what our partnership would look like and even had two different versions. The first version was the church version. This proposal was aimed at our Leadership Council. It had data, opportunities, and the SWOT analysis, but it also had Bible verses and a vision for how this partnership would help us become a church the community would miss.

The school version was the principal's version. We removed the Bible verses and faith elements and instead focused on potential benefits for the school community.

Higher test scores.

Caring adults in the building reading to children.

A partner that could help with needs that were beyond the scope of a school's budget.

Some may object that having two different plans was hypocritical or makes us guilty of the bait-and-switch tactics I bemoaned in Chapter 3.

Perhaps.

We were not trying to be disingenuous.

We were not trying to hide our lamp under a bushel.

We were trying hard to forge a third path of church-school partnership, and we were tying really hard to make sure we were setting up another example of the mission field model.

It can be tempting to get a vision for partnering with a school and simply email the principal, request a meeting, and share all your enthusiasm without any semblance of a plan.

It's good to have excitement.

It's great to have passion and a vision for the local public school.

It's better, though, to combine passion, excitement, and vision with data, research, and a plan. Educators—and specifically principals—are used to data, research, and plans. It's the language they speak and it's the quickest—and best—way to break through whatever initial objections they may have.

If a church can help answer questions they already have or meet needs they already know about, who's going to say no to that?

A New Leader

I met Jackie McNamara, Cleveland's new principal, on August 3, 2007. Little did either of us know how much our meeting would change both our lives and Hillcrest. Looking back at that first meeting, Jackie admits to being doubtful about the relationship.

She remembers "when Pastor Brian walked into my office at Cleveland in the summer of 2007 and told me that Hillcrest wanted to partner with Cleveland, I have to be honest and tell you I was doubtful about that relationship. In previous experiences the business partner relationship looked great on paper but just didn't really ever happen."

All the more reason why you need a plan going before you even meet with a school. The last thing you want is for your group or your church to be one of those previous partners that looked great on paper but failed to deliver what you put on the paper, or worse, what you said you were going to do but never even took the time or the effort to put on paper!

Jackie was open and receptive. We had a good first meeting, and landed on four initiatives:

- Reading buddies
- Mentors
- Resource drives
- Back to school lunch for the staff

This last one came from Jackie's desire to buy her staff lunch during one of the back to school work days since she is the new principal. There's no funding for this, and it's not feasible for a principal to simply buy lunch for 80 or so people.

We offered that Hillcrest would pick up the tab. Right in the meeting. Without knowing if there was even a budget for it!

I'm the first to admit this is a departure from my leadership style. Normally, I would have said we'd have to think about it and then I would go and ask for permission. For whatever reason, though, I thought this was a 'say yes now' kind of situation (or the kind of situation that at most would require "asking for forgiveness"!).

What I sensed God asking us to do in that first meeting with Jackie was to show some proof, give some evidence, that Hillcrest was serious about this partnership. We had a great plan, and we had great ideas, but we were more than just thoughts and ideas on paper. Jackie may have initially been doubtful about this new partnership; our desire to buy of the lunch gave immediate evidence that Hillcrest was serious in its desire to serve the school and be a church that would be missed.

Hillcrest has bought every back to school staff lunch since that day.

BRIAN STROH

Chapter 5: The Reveal

The impact on my faith was solidifying the truth I know and one reason I am at Hillcrest, which is to take the church outside of the walls, and it is right to do so. It reminded me that so many need Jesus and they are looking for Him but don't know where He is. He is in me, and I hope that they saw that and felt loved by me.

Deena Perry, reading buddy, mentor, and Pampered Chef consultant

Building a bridge to a local school was just one of several conversations Hillcrest was having during the summer of 2007. Pastor Doug and our other pastors were teaching about being Jesus in our community and how we could answer the question of being a church the community would miss. Our leadership was reading *The Church of Irresistible Influence* together and beginning to have life-changing conversations about what this could look like for Hillcrest.

Much has been written about generational poverty and how to overcome it. There are books such as *When Helping Hurts* and *Toxic Charity* that make good arguments for churches and non-profits to be careful in their poverty assistance and to make sure we don't do for others what others are capable to do themselves. That is solid and wise advice. The challenge with that advice is what to do with the children, who have not made decisions that have led to poverty and, without any intervention, any mentoring, or any training, will continue the cycle of generational poverty we want to see tackled. As a leadership and a church, we landed on the side of helping children. We would later learn some lessons that would sharpen and strengthen our helping—we didn't get it right all the time—but we wanted to be on the side of under-resourced children and assisting them in whatever way we could to give them the opportunity to no longer be 'under-resourced.'

We designated a Sunday in September as the day we would share our community focused outreach initiatives to the church, and we called it "The Reveal." In addition to being a business partner for Cleveland (the specific reveal projects would be reading buddies and mentors), we revealed additional partnerships including financially paying for adoptions, recruiting Hillcrest families to be foster parents, and launching an after-school tutoring program for under-resourced middle school students.

Another opportunity we revealed was Feeding South Dakota's Backpack Program. Feeding South Dakota had just launched a program to help feed under-resourced children on the weekend by sending home a backpack of food home to kids who received free meals at school. We got on the ground floor with this program and decided to sponsor its launch of 75 children at Cleveland. To date, Hillcrest has given close to $100,000—sponsoring 740 backpacks—to this ministry.

The Reveal is one of the most exciting periods of ministry I have ever been a part of.

The solidarity of our staff and leadership.

The energy we were pouring into the Scriptures and outside reading about being a church that the community would miss as palpable.

We were meeting with principals, non-profit executive directors, city and county leaders on how one normal church could best address these issues. The build-up, the excitement, and the energy leading up to and following the Reveal is perhaps the most impactful ministry we had done as a church in our 60 years of existence.

It was a day I almost missed.

Sick

In the midst of the excitement, energy, and work we were doing for the Reveal and becoming a church the community would miss, it was also a season of life with little care for myself.

I was working full-time as the ministry pastor at Hillcrest.

I was teaching a couple classes as an adjunct professor at Colorado Technical University.

Tarina and I had three boys under the age of 5, with Charley not yet 1.

Looking back, it was a pace I was not able to keep in the long term.

Or the short term.

A typical day that year included staying up late and then getting into the office by 5. My schedule was the source of energetic discussions with Tarina, and this pace was not good for my health. Like most people who were trying to build something great, I dug in.

I stated how much work there was to be done with the Reveal. I expressed that in addition to all of the reveal stuff, I was overseeing the block party and ministry fair—two of our bigger annual events that required time, energy, and several meetings.

I told one of the bigger lies out there and said, "Once this season passed, I'd put her words into practice."

The season never got the chance to pass.

I turned 30 that September. A couple days later, we headed to Tarina's folks to watch her little brother's homecoming game. I didn't feel well at all that morning and remember getting a smoothie to settle the stomach. At the dinner before the homecoming game, I didn't want a pulled pork sandwich—a true indication I really was not feeling well! The next day, Saturday, I was full on sick. Both ends. I was miserable. I stayed home from church on Sunday as it was still coming out both ends—it's the only Sunday I've missed due to illness in 15 years of ministry. Things got worse as the week began, as I couldn't keep anything down—I was throwing up water. Tuesday night Tarina called Pastor Doug to take me to the emergency room to figure out what was wrong with me. They ran some tests and couldn't really figure out anything specific—there was no diagnosis or anything. I was just really sick. They pumped some IV fluids into me and admitted me to the hospital where I stayed for a night before being discharged on Thursday. I lost over 20 pounds! I would feel better a bit each day and would be good enough to at least be present at Charley's first birthday party. My mom and both my sisters came down to help Tarina with the boys while I recovered.

Even 10 years later, it was such a very humbling time. I was incredibly disappointed and discouraged that I had missed out on the week's events leading up to the Reveal. Jackie mentioned that something must have been wrong with me as I hadn't replied to any emails that week. Looking back, I was making all of this community work Hillcrest was going to enter into about me. In the midst of communicating to our church that this church gig isn't about us, God was communicating that this brand-new partnership with Cleveland was not about me. I was supposed to be on stage helping interview Jackie and other community leaders to communicate the Reveal and instead was relegated to sitting in a chair and watching it all happen. I was totally taken out of the picture, as if to say this can and will happen without you.

I believe there's a time in every spiritual leader's development where you learn this fundamental lesson that it's not about you. Some of us probably get the opportunity to learn this lesson more than once. The irony is not lost on me that I was trending toward making all of this community work about me. I wanted to be a pastor—a worker—

my church would miss, and the goal of being a church the community would miss was the vehicle to get me there. My point is not to get too theological. One could say God caused my illness or God simply allowed natural cause and effect to take its course. Whatever the cause, my interpretation was a wake-up call.

A call to heed my wife's wisdom.

A call to take better care of myself.

A call that ministry—even partnering with a public school—is not about me.

The day of the Reveal was a tremendous day—one I will never forget. We combined services that day and guest after guest came on stage and communicated what Hillcrest's involvement with them would mean to their organization and to the community. You could feel the energy, the Spirit, moving within our church to set about to be a church that the community would miss. That day,

- Hillcrest sponsored 83 backpacks of food for the weekend for Cleveland's students, giving over $8,300 and making the backpack offering a tradition each fall. This offering was more than our normal weekly giving amount!
- Forty Hillcresters volunteered to serve as a reading buddy at Cleveland.
- Twenty Hillcresters volunteered to mentor a student at Cleveland through Lutheran Social Services' School-Based Mentoring Program, a program we discovered while working on the Reveal that was operating in several schools but had yet to make inroads at Cleveland.

For perspective, one-third of Hillcrest adults had volunteered to either be a reading buddy or a mentor!

The Reveal would be one of those events that fundamentally changed our church's mission, culture, and values. From that day on, every Hillcrester had a common event and common language to rally around answering the question of being a church the community would miss.

Chapter 6: Start Strong

"We have to underpromise and overdeliver when we are serving public schools. Because we are not proselytizing, it's our proclamation of who we are as Christ-followers that we follow up what we said we are going to do with excellence."

Mike Tenbusch, *The Jonathan Effect*

We wanted to start strong entering our first year of partnering with Cleveland. We wanted to say 'yes' to all that we could to demonstrate good faith to the school that we were serious about our end of the partnership and doing what we could to serve the staff and students of Cleveland. The first items to act on were to activate those who had volunteered to be a mentor or a reading buddy. I had to balance two very strong realities. First, I wanted to make sure we did right by Cleveland. It wasn't going to be much of a partnership if the staff and students didn't receive any benefit from it. Second, volunteering at Cleveland had to be a good experience for Hillcresters, especially those who were signing up for front-line service as a mentor or a reading buddy. These opportunities were outside most comfort zones, so it was imperative that our people felt like what they did mattered. We knew it would take some time from the Reveal to when our people got into Cleveland and started serving students, but we had to reduce the interim time as best we could. We had to take advantage of the energy the Reveal had produced and knew that if we waited too long, the energy would wane and we'd start off our partnership with Cleveland on a less than ideal foot.

Reading Buddies

The reading buddy program had the greatest amount of volunteer interest but would also prove to be a challenging project to get off the ground. There wasn't much paperwork required to be a reading buddy, and Cleveland didn't require any training (though we decided to offer some to our reading buddies)—the challenge was the administrative task of matching our reading buddies with teachers and classrooms on a schedule that made sense for both the volunteer and the teacher. It doesn't make much sense to have a reading buddy come to a classroom during math time or worse, when the class is out to gym or music. Our reading buddies had let me know what day they could serve, when during that day they could serve, and whether they had a preference in terms of the grade they volunteered with. Some reading buddies indicated great flexibility, while others were working in their volunteering over a lunch hour or before or after work. There were 40 reading buddies, which meant 40 schedules to work with and try to communicate to Cleveland. We also knew it wouldn't be fair to dump this administrative task on Cleveland's leadership. If we wanted our people into the building as soon as possible, we were going to have to assist with the placement of reading buddies. That's not meant as a slight to Cleveland or its staff; it's the reality that in the scope of a school day or week, the challenge of helping outside volunteers get into a building isn't going to be at the top of anyone's to-do list.

Tenbusch alludes to this when he writes

> One of the biggest challenges to the work is that many school leaders and teachers "don't" get volunteers. Most educators have been trained to succeed in a control-and-command environment. The principal controls the teachers. The teachers control their students. They are both focused on making it through the end of the day so they can go home and check papers or prepare lessons plans for the next day. They are not thinking about how to get more people to come

into their school; that only adds more variables to an already overextended day. Therefore, schools with huge needs for caring volunteers may not seem receptive to them. This is why it's important to look for ways your church can make a meaningful difference for a school early in the courtship phase.

(p. 146)

We got Jackie's blessing to put the program together.

We were given the building's daily schedules and knew what classes were in recess, what classes were in specials, and when.

We were given a typical outline of each grade's schedules and knew when fifth grade did math and when first grade did reading.

We were given access and the ability to contact teachers and serve as a reading buddy realtor of sorts, matching our reading buddy with a classroom that made sense based on the reading buddy's schedule and the teacher's schedule.

Once we found a match, we'd email both the teacher and the reading buddy, introducing them to one another, and then they would communicate with each other on when to start. This wasn't exactly in my formal Hillcrest job description (though to be fair, much of what I do isn't detailed in a job description!), and I was soon taking this work home and working on it after the kids went to bed or in the morning before anyone was awake. It was the kind of work where you knew you were instantly making a difference, or at least knowing it had the potential to make a difference. I was able to utilize skills that had served me well in my church work and now use them to help us connect our people with a local school. It was a lot of fun to watch the email replies come in from teachers who affirmed that the day and time would work for them.

Thanks for the Feedback

The next important piece concerning the reading buddy ministry was follow-up. It's probably the most important step whenever you're launching a new ministry or program. Follow-up was extremely important, as both Cleveland and Hillcrest were trying to get a sense of each other. In my initial 'realtor' email between the teacher and the Hillcrester, I wrote that I would meet the Hillcrester over at Cleveland at the first meeting to show her around and formally introduce her to the teacher. I also made sure to follow up with the reading buddy after her first time in the classroom and also after she had served a few times to see if there were any problems, see how things were going, and also see what we could be doing to make sure her volunteering experience was the best that it could be.

Follow-up is a tremendous opportunity at a leader's disposal. I get it. Leaders are busy people, and those who work in churches often have a hard-enough time filling their ministries with volunteers that there isn't much time for follow-up. There's also the reality that while we may be interested in the feedback, we know the greater priority is filling the volunteer role regardless of whether that volunteer role is actually a good fit for a person.

We tell ourselves that we'd like to know what Susie thinks about working with middle school girls, but if she doesn't like it, that's one more problem for us. And whether Susie likes it or not, I need someone to work with middle school girls. So better to keep Susie with middle school girls than risk feedback and have to do something with it.

We knew this had to be a great fit for the teacher and the classroom. We knew if we lost there, the partnership would be damaged and our credibility would be challenged. We also knew if it wasn't a good fit for the Hillcrester, we would lose a volunteer and also lose 'word of mouth' when it came time to highlight the ministry or recruit additional volunteers. We needed feedback from both sources to work out any initial kinks that we discovered early in the partnership.

Some of the kinks were easy fixes. Hillcresters were getting back to me and indicating a positive overall experience. One of the more common critiques from volunteers was they were not actually helping with reading. While the concept of a reading buddy was a newer idea, it's not the first time that volunteers had been inside a classroom. More seasoned teachers were having our volunteers do other things—helping with math, cutting out laminating, making copies—that they decided would be most helpful to them. Nothing wrong with that at all, except for the dissonance our volunteers would experience when they anticipated reading with an under-resourced first grader only to be cutting out laminating for a half-hour. We would not have discovered that information without follow-up, and it was an easy fix. Sometimes the Hillcrester wanted to do what was best for the teacher, and if that meant cutting laminating or making copies, so be it; the Hillcrester was happy to help. In other instances, the Hillcrester preferred time with a student or students, and in those cases, we reached out to the teacher with the Hillcrester's preference, and the teacher was more than willing to make that work.

A second kink was the interaction between Hillcresters and the front office staff. Jackie would periodically check in with me to see how things were going with Hillcresters, and one of the things she would always inquire about was how the front office was doing. When I followed up with Hillcresters, I discovered the reason behind Jackie's question. I heard from a few Hillcresters that they felt like a nuisance to the staff when they arrived at Cleveland. There wasn't much of a greeting or acknowledgment of our volunteers' presence.

I can understand the front office's perspective. We were new to the building. There's no telling that we would not be some flash in the pan for that year and then fizzle out. As Tenbusch writes, we were to expect some resistance at the beginning of the relationship.

From our volunteers' perspective, though, it presented unnecessary tension to an action that already required some tension to begin with. It wasn't the easiest thing in the world for our volunteers to take part of their day, take time away from work, and volunteer at this school they had little relationship with. The neutral at best—and unfriendly at worst—greeting the volunteers would receive did not help volunteers get over their initial fears of service—it only heightened them!

Quick rant—often the first person in an organization a customer or a volunteer deals with is the front office staff—an administrative assistant, a secretary, a customer service representative. These staff are the ones who answer the phone and greet you at the door. It's simply good business sense for an organization to make sure they have kind and service-oriented people in these positions. It's inexpensive marketing, for the positive feelings these staff are able to pass onto customers, clients, and volunteers only help the organization's overall impression. As a principal and leader, Jackie knew this important truth.

Over the course of that first year, the interaction between Hillcresters and the front office staff greatly improved. Looking back, it seems almost comical that this was even an issue as the front office staff are great—extremely helpful and welcoming. Our consistent presence within the school no doubt has helped as well.

Mentors

Our second initiative within Cleveland was providing mentors. Our newly formed partnership with Lutheran Social Services' School-Based Mentoring Program served as the conduit for mentors to be matched with Cleveland students. The school-based mentoring program required applications, background checks, and training for someone to serve as a mentor—all good things! But we wanted to again shorten the time between when the volunteers signed up to getting them paired with a student. To quicken the process, we brought the applications to Hillcrest and had interested people complete them there. LSS graciously offered to provide mentor training at Hillcrest on Sunday after worship services, and we hosted two such events that fall. Some pastors may disagree, but I am a strong proponent of leveraging when people are already at your facility. If you can provide lunch and care for children, you can take care of a training or a meeting after Sunday services and not have to ask people to come back at some other point during the week.

The goal of school-based mentoring was to match a caring adult with a Cleveland student whom the counselor would identify as someone who would benefit from a mentor. The students often exhibited some behavior that the staff felt a mentor could address: school attendance, school performance, behavioral issues within the classroom. The students often came from under-resourced backgrounds, and most with only one parent at home. The opportunity for Hillcresters was to be a caring adult who would show up each week over the student's lunch hour, have lunch with the student, and spend the lunch recess with him or her playing a game, going out to the playground, working on a project, or helping with schoolwork. The key ingredient in the mentoring relationship was consistency. When Hillcresters signed up to be a mentor, they were making a weekly commitment—same day, same time, same place. Research—and stories revealed from Cleveland's staff—revealed many of the students did not have the benefit of consistency in any relationship with an adult.

Our mentors knew this going in and understood the biggest potential challenge with the student would be weathering the 'testing phase' when the student would test the relationship to see if the adult would stick or not. Some students were ecstatic to have a mentor and some tested the relationship.

The student might ask for a friend to come with during the mentor time.

The student might not want to do anything during the mentor time.

The student might communicate that she did not need a mentor or tell the mentor to not come back—that one happened to me!

Those experiences 'pop the clutch.' Mentors are taking a risk—similar to the reading buddy—and taking time away from work, leaving their comfort zone, and entering into an unknown environment to do something they feel God is calling them to do. In the mentor's psyche, it's a situation ripe with excuses for why it will not work. Pair those fears and anxieties with the mentee saying he doesn't need you or want to spend time with you, and that's a recipe for failure! The initial feedback from the mentee experiences experienced in the 'testing phase' only served to fuel the mentors' doubts.

The mentors who made it through that testing phase often got to experience the sweet spot of the relationship. Hillcrest had mentors who became official Big Brothers and Sisters to their students, meaning they could continue the mentoring relationship outside of the school day and building. Pastor Doug was one such mentor who began a mentoring relationship with a student that grew into his being the mentor's Big Brother. Eventually, because of home issues for the student, Pastor Doug and his wife, Jenny, eventually became the student's foster parents and provided shelter and a home for his mentee for over a year and a half. It was an incredible experience and privilege to watch as Hillcrest's most senior leader truly and radically lived out what we as a church were trying to do. The credibility of Pastor Doug's actions and lifestyle spoke loud to our church. This movement wasn't going to be something we preached about, talked about, but then left to the people in the pews to accomplish. This movement was being spearheaded by our leader, and we were going to follow him in this endeavor of being a church that the community would radically miss.

It's Leadership 101 to underscore the importance of the senior leader and leadership team being on board for this type of ministry, this type of movement. If senior leadership isn't on board—or simply views this ministry as 'one more' ministry within a church like student or children's ministries—it's a setup for conflict and frustration. Leadership will try to fit this type of ministry into its existing structure, probably deciding on outreach as the best place. Leadership will try to designate some resources—both financial and human—to this type of ministry on a limited and 'trial' basis to see if it's viable before making a bigger investment. While this type of thinking is prudent and comes straight from business and ministry best practices, this type of thinking would not have benefited our start-up with Cleveland. This type of ministry requires an all-in approach, from the top of the leadership chain to the rest of the church. We were not going to become the type of church the community would miss by making incremental steps. We were going to become the type of church the community would miss by starting strong and then going all in.

BRIAN STROH

Chapter 7: All In

At Cleveland I have served through reading buddies, mentoring, painting playground equipment, landscaping, teacher lunches, cards and gifts to teachers. All of these have gone well as a result of the leadership at Cleveland and a church that has not made any missteps with proselytizing. The work at Cleveland has helped me see that the church can love without expecting something in return. So often the church is looking for a commitment or a change from those we serve, but at Cleveland I have seen Hillcrest love for the sake of love.

Pastor Doug Bartel, lead pastor of Hillcrest Church

History tells us that in 1519 Cortes, upon landing in Veracruz to begin his great conquest, ordered his men to "burn the ships," implying that one of two things was going to happen: They were going to conquer this newfound land, or they were going to die trying. There was no plan B.

No contingency plan.

No chance to retreat if things started not going well.

Five years prior to our relationship with Cleveland, Hillcrest purchased 58 acres out on Sioux Falls' eastern edge. It was a barren piece of dirt with a car lot for a neighbor but not much else. The city was booming, though, and much of the growth was sprawling around our land. It made perfect sense.

As a church, we were booming.

Three services.

A growing children's ministry.

A small group ministry where hundreds of Hillcresters came out each Sunday evening for a meal and then small groups.

An attractive and energetic youth ministry.

Our leadership believed we had outgrown our current facility, and that if we were to continue to grow, we needed more space.

We considered numerous options.

We discussed buying out the homes that bordered our property.

We looked at buying the old Sioux Falls Christian High School.

We decided against those options and instead pursued a new location with a new building.

We met with consultants.

We organized capital campaigns.

We hosted fundraising events.

We collected offerings.

We bought land and looked forward to the time of a new facility with more space to do more ministry.

And then the Reveal happened.

Our pastoral staff, our leadership team, and our church no longer felt good about an extended campaign to build a new building for ourselves.

Our team didn't feel good about the existing debt that we had on our current facility and then knowing we'd be adding to that amount and length of time.

Our team didn't feel good communicating on Sundays that we were about the community and then game-planning through the week that we were really about ourselves as we sought plans for a new building.

We knew we had to sell our land.

Burn the bridges.

It wouldn't be until early 2008 that we would list the land.

2008.

The year of the Great Recession.

The year of the worst financial crisis since the Great Depression.

The year when housing prices fell 31%.

The year the government took over Fannie Mae and Freddie Mac and bailed out the likes of AIG and others.

This was the market, the environment, in which we were going to sell our 58 acres of land, pay off our existing mortgage, and use the remaining monies to fund our reveal efforts.

To give it away.

To burn the ships.

When selling something, it only takes one buyer, and we were able to find a buyer. The buyer ended up paying about $30,000 per acre. We had paid $12,500 per acre five years before.

The result was a tidy profit of just over a million dollars. That's an ROI of 19%.

In the worst economic year our country has experienced since the Great Depression.

How do you explain that?

How do you explain being able to sell that land in a significantly down economy where every pundit and expert would tell you that you're crazy to try and unload that property at that time?

Another 'looking back' moment—or series of moments—where we clearly saw God at work, moving us and shaping us to be a community that the community would miss and providing an abundance of funding to continue to provide answers to that question.

Go Big

Our relationship with Cleveland was growing. Our volunteers were consistent in their serving. Student were looking forward to the weekly appearance of their reading buddies and mentors. The teachers and staff were seeing our presence as a benefit, and we were showing that we were in this relationship for the long term.

As a church, we hold an event that recognizes and appreciates our volunteers each spring. We typically take over a restaurant—or most of it(!)—pay for the volunteers' (and their families') meal, provide something for the kids to do, and give away prizes. Hillcrest is blessed with so many people who volunteer their time and talent to serve God within our church, and this new partnership with Cleveland meant they were now also volunteering outside of our church. For the volunteer appreciation event the spring of the first year we had connected with Cleveland, we invited Jackie, the principal, and Emily Lafrentz, then a kindergarten teacher, to share about the impact Hillcresters had on the school in that first year. It was another meaningful moment in a year full of them and a remarkable reminder that at a church event, we had a principal and a teacher speaking to our volunteers!

In our initial conversations with Jackie, we had asked her what her dreams were for the school. What were things would she want to do if money were no object? It was this conversation where we began to sponsor the catered lunch for the staff for their back to school meeting, the first idea to arise from this discussion.

A second idea from that discussion were T-shirts for the school for a Super Reader reading program. We unfortunately had to pass on that idea, as great as it was, as we were not quite set up operationally to fund such initiatives. We had not yet sold our land and had yet to budget any operating funds for our support of Cleveland.

The third idea to come from the discussion would be big, really big, and come at just the right time for both organizations.

Cleveland's Parent Teacher Association (PTA) had been trying to raise funds for computers for Cleveland. The school had no designated computer lab due to every available space being used for classrooms, and this was years before the Sioux Falls School District would put a Chromebook in the hands of every third- through 12th-grade student. The PTA's annual fundraiser would do well; it would bring in about $6,000 or so each year. The challenge with that amount was two-fold. First, at an estimate of $60,000, it would take about 10 years for the PTA to raise enough money. Second, those fund-raising funds also supported other areas such as back to school Bingo, teacher appreciation, and the end of year field day complete with inflatables! Jackie knew all this and mentioned it to us in our early conversations about a big thing we could do for Cleveland. She knew her school would never get a computer lab nor have computers at Cleveland, given the current circumstances.

Jackie asked Hillcrest for 60 laptops. The laptops would be broken into two mobile computers labs, each with 30 laptops. She envisioned the laptops being on carts and able to move around the building. She saw the mobile labs being used by teachers in classrooms when it tied in with a certain lesson or curriculum.

It was a big ask.

She knew it was a big ask, but she also knew if she didn't ask, if she didn't say anything, that she might be missing out on an opportunity to better her school community. There was obviously no way she could have known that at the time of her asking about computers that Hillcrest had decided to sell land, pay off debt, and give the rest of the money away. There was obviously no way she could have known that after paying off debt and paying capital gains taxes, that Hillcrest would have close to a million dollars in the bank that it had designated to give away to the community.

We ran the idea through the chain of command. Our staff was on board. We took it to the Leadership Council, and after some discussion, they too were on board and gave the green light. We had a business meeting in early August—the week before teachers were to report to school for their back to school meetings—and made the proposal to our membership. We asked our church to approve giving Cleveland $58,000 for two mobile computer labs.

The whole concept, the whole idea, still gives me pause almost 10 years later. Education and education funding are full of arm-chair quarterbacks who think they could manage school district budgets and funding better than those who do. Some elected local and state officials bemoan the current reality of education spending and propose tax hikes or other programs to help funnel more funds to education. Other elected officials say the schools have enough money, that teachers are already adequately compensated, and that if a school or district is in need of something, it's evidence that funds are being misused or misappropriated.

As a church and leadership, we tried our best to stay out of those conversations. We trusted Jackie and what she was telling us. There were no district funds allocated for computers at Cleveland. We could challenge the fairness or the rightness of such a decision, but it didn't change the fact that Cleveland wasn't getting computers from the district.

Hillcrest's membership overwhelmingly and enthusiastically approved the request. It set up for a very fun week!

We first made the call to Jackie, a fun call to make, and told her the news.

Wednesday, three days after the business meeting, we were already planning to be at Cleveland for the back to school meeting, and so we decided to have Pastor Doug share the news with the teachers and staff as they gathered right before lunch. It was an incredible moment as Pastor Doug made the announcement, watching the emotion spread throughout the room. You could just see and feel the reaction. When Pastor Doug was finished speaking, the whole room was standing in applause.

This moment did so many things for our partnership with Cleveland:

- It solidified us as a business partner that was committed for the long-term. We weren't going to be here for a year and then run when things got a bit hard or uncomfortable.
- It established trust between us and Jackie as well as the rest of the school. WE had delivered on the school's biggest possible ask. While we mutually understood that we may not be able to say 'yes' to every ask or an ask of this magnitude in the near future, we had come through on the biggest thing the school needed. It's difficult to communicate the trust that comes from such a decision. We were truly committed to this school, this community, and being a church the community would miss.
- It provided a benchmark for future decisions. The computer labs for Cleveland gave our leadership and church a reference point when we would make even bigger financial decisions, such as planting a farm and drilling a well in South Sudan ($75,000) and the even more incredible Jubilee, where each Hillcrest family received an envelope with $500 to either give to an organization they supported, to a family in need, or their own needs. The Jubilee would cost Hillcrest $100,000!

These decisions would have been much more difficult had we not made the Cleveland computer lab decision.

- It presented us with a picture of what a church could look like. For many, church is what happens on Sunday mornings and, to an extent, Wednesday nights. Church in this perspective is singing songs and listening to a message. In our desire to be a church that the community would miss, we desired to make these types of decisions to demonstrate what a church could look like. We wanted to move away from church simply being what happened within our walls and move to church being what happened outside of our walls.

Chapter 8: Messy Ministry

Hillcrest nurtured (my) desire to be more of a servant! The support from Hillcrest as our business partner was amazing! Numerous times the gift of a notecard with a prayer helped ground me when there may have been a sense of spiraling downward. I hung all of those note cards up in my office as a constant visual reminder that people were praying for our students as well as our staff. There was never a time when we reached out with a need and it wasn't met with your kindness and generosity. My faith was strengthened by your constant reminders of your presence in our school, and that will never be forgotten.

Kristie Schreck, former Cleveland librarian

Full disclosure: this kind of ministry is messy.

I want to be able to write that the students of every reading buddy raised their standardized test scores.

That every mentee steered clear of poor life decisions because of his or her mentor's constant caring influence.

That every teacher felt an overwhelming sense of purpose to stay in a challenging school environment because of Hillcrest.

There were small—and eventually, bigger—wins. One day a reading buddy called to say that the student she read with, in the course of reading, spontaneously asked her a question about Jesus and who he was! It was incredible to have this question come so soon in our partnership, and we saw it as evidence that we were where God wanted us.

For every moment like that, there were 2–3 moments of mess.

A mentor wasn't clicking with a student.

A reading buddy wasn't clicking with the classroom.

A reading buddy felt she was more an interruption to the class than a benefit.

A mentor—me(!)—whose mentor would tell him that he didn't need him there and would prefer to not have a mentor.

A mentor wanted to know what to do with her student who didn't have appropriate winter clothing.

A mentor who wanted to know if she should follow her student who was switching schools or if she should begin with a new student. She was worried about switching to a different school and whether that would count!

There is a temptation to interpret the presence of messiness as proof there's a problem with the mission. I certainly understand the temptation. I, like many Hillcresters, initially believed simply showing up would be all it took to win over the building and school. If we simply showed up, good things would happen.

This type of thinking, though, is misguided. It views the relationship through the lens of 'what can we (Hillcrest) do for you (Cleveland)?' rather than how we can both serve and benefit each other. No one likes to be used, and while it may seem harsh to think of it this way, even an under-resourced school would be hesitant in entering into a partnership with a church if the guise was so the church could feel better about itself. It may not look like usury, but it is, no matter how dressed up it looked.

The presence of messy situations served as a challenge for us as a church to make it through that 'trial phase' in our partnership with Cleveland. Institutionally, we were somewhat being challenged to see if we would lean in, endure the mess, and be a consistent partner.

I Don't Want That Coat

Winter provided an opportunity to demonstrate our commitment and lean into some discomfort. South Dakota winters are harsh. Many of Cleveland's students didn't have the necessary gear needed for sub-zero days.

Some students came to school without hats and gloves.

Some students came to school with boots and coats that had clearly seen better days.

We decided to spearhead a winter clothing drive for Cleveland students who needed gear. On paper, it was a simple process. Cleveland's teachers would identify students in their classrooms with a need for winter clothing. They then emailed that information over to me, letting me know sizes and gender. We took that information and designed a bulletin board where Hillcresters could sponsor winter gear for a student.

A Hillcrester might take a tag for size 3 boys' boots and a 14-16 winter coat for a girl. Hillcresters would pick up the items and drop them off at Hillcrest, and we'd take over the clothing for Cleveland's counseling and administrative staff to deliver to the students.

This was certainly felt like a win-win situation! Hillcresters got the opportunity to minister in a financial way to students. Students who didn't have winter clothing got winter clothing. Everyone gets to feel good about what was going on, right?!

Messy. This type of ministry is messy.

Jackie called shortly after our first couple of trips of dropping off the donated winter gear. There was a problem. Some students were not happy with the winter gear they were receiving. They wondered if they could exchange a black coat in for a purple one like their friend received. They wondered if they could receive the same style of boots that a younger sibling had received. We inadvertently created a class system through our winter gear donation! Some students received higher end or more expensive items then other students. What was supposed to be a blessing to the community ended up creating a problem and unnecessary conflict. While the book *Toxic Charity* (and others) hadn't been written yet, I imagined it was this type of scenario that served as inspiration!

For this first drive, there was little we could do. The clothing was donated, and true to Hilllcrest fashion, we had gone over and above what was needed. The first part of my discussion with Jackie was shock and maybe even some anger. I'll be the first to confess that I thought the only emotion one should have when getting something free was gratitude. I will also confess thoughts went through my head such as that the gear we had donated to Cleveland was newer and nicer than what my children were wearing, as my thrifty and resourceful wife scoured hand-me-downs and thrift stores for our children's winter gear. Who were these students to complain about getting something new when the day or two before they had nothing?

The second part of our conversation focused on how we might do this next year.

That was hopeful, I guess, that Jackie envisioned doing this a next year!

Maybe next year we collected gently used clothing.

Maybe next year Hillcresters donated gift cards or funds and then Cleveland and Hillcrest worked together on purchasing the clothing to make sure there weren't real or perceived differences among the clothing that students would be picking from.

Maybe next year. While I had given Cleveland a problem that it did not need, I was hopeful that I was having a conversation with the principal that contained the words 'maybe next year.'

Other Messes

Cleveland wasn't the only area where we would experience this type of messy ministry. Something we learned quickly (that under-resourced people know too well) is the fact there isn't much incentive, at least in the short-term, for under-resourced people to increase their incomes. When an under-resourced family moves up slightly in income, they no longer qualify for food stamps and other government programs meant to assist folks just like them. We worked with one family through a program called the Genesis Project, a program where mentors come alongside families to support them in their attempt to become more financially and domestically stable. The husband was a cook for a newer downtown restaurant. He made decent money, but not enough where he didn't qualify for food stamps. His boss wanted to promote him to an assistant manager, which would mean more pay, but the pay increase would have been a setback for him and his family, as it would have kicked him off of food stamps—a win from most conservatives' perspectives—but the pay increase was not enough to make up the difference. He was a smart man and knew staying at the lower job and the lower wage was worth it because he was making more there then if he took the pay increase.

At times likes this we can get a bit haughty, or dare I say even self-righteous, and say that the man should have taken the promotion, because it could lead to another promotion (or at least to skills and experience that would come in handy for future jobs and opportunities). Fair enough. But look at it from the man's perspective, without the benefit of the perspective that we come from. The government and society were providing a disincentive for this man to make more money. They were sending the signal that it was better to stay where you are because you will make more there then if you 'move up.' There was no graduated level for food stamps or public assistance—it is all or nothing.

We also began to understand differences between our way of thinking and the perspective of those we were partnering with. I can remember telling more than one mentee family that they had better (more expensive) cable television packages than I had. At first, this and other discoveries troubled our people. They would partner with an under-resourced family and discover huge televisions in their homes but little food in their refrigerators. It was hard for many—myself included—to hide our middle-class disgust.

How could so-and-so afford a 60-inch TV but not have milk in the fridge?

How could so-and-so afford satellite television or the premium cable package and have kids running around in rags?

Here Ruby Payne again proved invaluable. Those in generational poverty view life from a short-term perspective. They do not have the benefit of experience with long-term thinking or strategies. They view life in the short-term, and thus from that perspective, it makes complete sense to spend a disproportionate amount of income on entertainment.

We finally came to understand all you can really do when mentoring with someone from an under-resourced situation is provide options and allow mentees to decide what's best for them and their families. Most of us from a middle-class or upper middle-class mindset are used to a goal-setting approach. You're in debt? Ok, then we need to do X, Y, and Z in order to get out of debt. It took time and experience to learn that it wasn't going to work like that. Instead, our approach would have to be more options based, where we as mentors would make suggestions and then allow the mentees the power to decide which, if any, of the options they wanted to implement in their lives.

One of the more colorful stories was a family where the wife worked full-time at a call center while the husband struggled to find gainful employment. His search for work was common to others, who like to search for work but have a reason as to why such and such a job didn't work. The couple had two children—a middle school daughter and a preschool-aged son. The rationale for the husband not working was so he could care for the son and save money on daycare. Fair enough. We did say at the onset that once the son was school aged—the upcoming school year—that he would need to resume the search for employment. The wife, in addition to working full time, also worked part time with her home-based business. It was a rather unique business in that she didn't sell cosmetics or cooking supplies but rather sold sex toys and other elements designed to spice up a couple's romantic relationship! It was a completely legitimate and legal business and her target markets were bachelorette parties and couples where the flame was dwindling a bit! In one of the weirdest things in my entire life, I said words I never thought I'd say when I told the wife, "Well, we need to see if you can set up some more sex parties!" We all laughed, but the idea was true nonetheless, that for this couple to get bill collectors off their back and move to a more solid future for their two children, they needed more money, along with some cutting of expenses, and in their current toolbox, this was the most likely way to bring in more money!

Messy ministry to say the least.

Outside Looking In

The first year of the Reveal was exciting and successful.

We had begun a mostly successful partnership with Cleveland.

We had financially paid for three adoptions.

Our gym was being used for an after-school club as other sites throughout town were too full and kids needed a place to go after school.

If you were a reading buddy, mentor, or on leadership at Hillcrest, you could feel the excitement and knew that God was up to something within our midst. You were on the front lines—the ground floor—of witnessing a church slowly change into one the community would miss.

The problem was: what if you were not on leadership or were not a mentor or not a reading buddy?

You felt like a spectator at a sporting event.

You cheered on your team.

You sensed your team was winning.

You knew you supported a winning team.

But you felt this gnawing sensation of wanting to be on the team.

To be where the action was.

To not just be a spectator.

More evidence that this is messy ministry was splitting the church into those who were active with at Cleveland and those who were watching or hearing about people serve at Cleveland.

For some, this is probably OK. My hunch is there will always be spectators within a church, or really anything in life—those who are content to watch. Content to know they belong to something exciting but never really invest themselves with the effort. We would hear this sentiment from several families looking to join us in membership. Repeatedly, prospective members would rave about how cool it was to attend a church that was for the community. Often, these prospective members failed to join in the efforts.

Many of our people, though, were frustrated in a good way. They were passionate about Cleveland. They believed in the Reveal's initiatives. They simply could not participate.

Some were not able to get away from work during the school day.

Some worked too far away from Cleveland to make a reading buddy or mentoring work. If you get an hour lunch break, spend 40 minutes in the car driving to and fro, it doesn't make for a successful serving opportunity.

Some could not line up their availability with Cleveland's availability.

We kept hearing this critique. Hillcresters wanted to join in on the action, get in the game, but couldn't because the game was being played at a time that wasn't ever going to work for them. While we kept highlighting our efforts at Cleveland and praising those who were involved, we were causing those on the outside to feel like losers without even having the ability to play the game.

So we added a second game.

Wednesday Night Service

We called it Wednesday Night Service.

I know—not the most original name! Never been good at the 'naming a program' thing. When I was a green youth pastor, we did a monthly youth ministry worship evening event we called 'Eden.' When we launched the Powerhouse Tutoring Center (more on this later), my original name was Whittier Neighborhood Tutoring Center because it was located in the Whittier Neighborhood. So catchy.

The spirit behind Wednesday Night Service was to provide a second opportunity for people to join in the excitement of the Reveal. If the school day schedule at Cleveland didn't work for you, or you weren't feeling called to adopt a child or become a foster care parent, Wednesday Night Service was created to give you the opportunity to participate in serving the community and becoming the kind of church that the community would miss.

In order to pull off Wednesday Night Service, we needed to cut our midweek children's programming. Easier said than done. While we had cut AWANA a couple years prior to the Reveal, we had replaced it with a different program for children. We had to free people to switch from volunteering at that program and instead participate in this program. We offered a meal ahead of time to make it an easier evening for our families. The families would sign up for a service opportunity that would take them into the community to be the church. There were numerous and diverse opportunities, including:

- Serving supper at the St. Francis House, a local homeless shelter.
- Organizing and cleaning at the Volunteers of America Thrift Store, where we helped transform the storefront and make it a viable thrift store option in Sioux Falls. Volunteers of America would later nominate Hillcrest as a Helpline Community Partner of the Year.
- Picking up and delivering furniture for the Furniture Mission.

It is important that organizations—including churches—'flesh out' their values. Many organizations—churches included—have mission statements, visions, and core values. These statements were crafted in boardrooms or staff meetings, put on letterheads and web sites, and presented to customers or members as the thing or things the organization is all about.

In church life, you value what you program.

Exhibit A is the worship service. Whether it's Sunday mornings, Saturday evenings, or sometime throughout the week, most if not all churches come together weekly for corporate worship. Music and singing, offering, prayer, and preaching are the most common elements of a typical worship service.

We program a worship service because we value it.

We spend money, hire staff, put it on the calendar, and measure the service's effectiveness all because the worship service is a value for a church. It may not be specifically stated or written down anywhere, but it is a value because we feed it time, money, and attention.

The same can be said for children's and student ministries in most churches. Again, whether stated or implicit values, these ministries are key values because they receive time, money, and attention.

Being a church that serves its community—being a church that the community would miss—can also be a value, but like the other values, it too requires time, money, and attention for it to truly be a key value within the church.

You can say you're a church that serves the community.

You can put it in your mission statement.

You can put it on the web site.

You can even preach about it and get people inspired to do it.

But—you have to actually do it.

You actually have to commit time, money, and attention to serving the community if it's actually going to become a value.

Wednesday Night Service was continuing to shift the paradigm for our church. We were not going to add it on as another ministry opportunity and only highlight it every so often. Wednesday Night Service codified service to the community as one of Hillcrest's most important values, because we fed it time, money, and attention.

Wednesday Night Service also provided interested Hillcresters the opportunity to partner with Cleveland in some new and exciting ways. For instance, each fall and spring we write out affirmation cards to every Cleveland staff member. Each staff member receives a card with a unique handwritten note from three or four Hillcresters.

The notes say things like:

- We're praying for you
- We hope you have a great year (in the fall)
- We hope you finish the year strong (in the spring)
- Thank you for all you do

Each note also contains a small gift card to places such as Target, Starbucks, the local grocery store, or Dairy Queen. Teaching is somewhat of a thankless profession, and even more so in an under-resourced environment. The gift cards are small—no one at Cleveland mistakes what Hillcrest gives as a bonus!

It's simply a way for our church to build another bridge into the school community.

It's a way for our church to provide a little bit of support and appreciation to those on the front line doing incredibly difficult and challenging work.

On Wednesday evenings, Hillcresters also served Cleveland with clerical work, removing graffiti off of playground equipment, painting playground equipment, picking up trash around the school, doing landscaping around the school, and preparing meals for fall and spring conferences.

Wednesday Night Service was a vehicle we used to ask the question: "How can we help?" While at times the results were messy, we wanted to continue to ask the school and its staff: "How can we help make your school community better?"

Chapter 9: Measuring Success

I have been a reading buddy at Cleveland for the last seven years. I have seen the kids grow immensely in the area of reading and comprehension. It has certainly been a privilege to partner with (my teacher) in this endeavor, and I would encourage all the body of Christ to engage in this process in some capacity!

Jason Lounsbery, discipleship elder at Hillcrest

Measuring success is critical when determining how successful you are at the goal you're trying to achieve.

Duh.

Churches are no different than sports teams, businesses, or schools. Churches want to know how they are doing.

Can we do better?

Are we winning?

What does it even mean for our church to win?

Reggie McNeal talks about the importance of churches changing their scorecards. He has written about the concept in books such as *The Present Future* and during conference sessions and seminars. The gist of the idea begins with the acknowledgment that most churches have two metrics they focus on: worship attendance and weekly giving. These two metrics tell us if we are succeeding or not. If we're winning or not.

We can then compare those metrics against other churches.

Churches in our community.

Churches with similar demographics.

Churches in our denomination.

We can compare when we talk with other pastors or friends who attend a different church to see how we stack up. We can look back at the previous year and if see if either or both of those two metrics have increased.

If they have, we celebrate!

If they haven't, we double down efforts to understand why not and work at raising them,

If they're stagnant, we often react the same as if they haven't grown.

Attendance and money—the only two metrics we use to measure success and effectiveness in church ministry.

Hillcrest was no different. We measured those metrics and based our success (or lack thereof) on those two scorecards. We had over 10 years of data for both metrics and could tell how we were doing historically at any given time. We even knew what months were bigger attendance or giving months (October and April) and what months were lower for attendance or giving (June, July, and August, no surprises there!).

Similar with many churches, we also printed the previous week's stats in the Sunday bulletin:

- Last week's attendance
- Last week's giving
- Year-to-date giving (essentially, the 'are we on budget?' statistic)

Who really knows why these statistics even made into the bulletin in the first place?

Maybe it was an attempt to keep people informed.

Maybe it was an attempt to communicate success to people who were attending the church (I admit I have often imagined a newcomer attending worship, seeing the stat that we're on budget for the year, and mentally going, 'Cool. This is a place where I want to keep coming back to, because hey, they are on budget!').

When we discussed the issue with our leadership, the most common reason given for why giving numbers were in the bulletin on a weekly basis was this: if there was a lower giving week, or year-to-date giving was below budget, then that information would inspire additional giving.

Seriously.

The idea was that we put the giving numbers in. When they're lower than what we need (which was often the case), people would see the lower number, realize their giving was now needed (in contrast to the rare times of surplus when it was then somehow not needed), and thus put more in the plate as it passed by.

Ironically, we never worried about the opposite effect. Of the rare week when we would surpass our weekly need and think 'Oh no, we better not put the really high number in the bulletin for this week because people will think we don't need their money and thus opt to hold onto it for the week.'

In over 15 years of ministry, I have yet to meet a person whose motivation to give was based on how well or not well the church was doing on a week-to-week basis. Sure, I know folks who would give a larger amount periodically or increase their giving during leaner times for the church. That motivation was more out of a relationship with the church and what God was asking them to do, not a response to a number in the bulletin. It was also rare that we'd get a higher-than-average week following a lower week, shooting additional holes in the theory that the lower giving number was a motivator for people.

Perhaps this was a holdover from old-school church thinking.

Perhaps someone thought it was cool and decided to put it in.

Perhaps once it made its way in the bulletin, we had to invent a rationale for why it was in the bulletin.

I don't really know. I do know that when we decided to remove those numbers from the bulletin, we had to answer several 'why' questions from people who really valued that information and wanted to see it each and every week.

The decision to remove the giving and attendance numbers from the weekly bulletin paved the way for our eyes and attention to focus on different scorecards.

Did we—and do we—still track attendance and weekly offering? Of course!

Do we use these metrics to determine our effectiveness and success? Of course.

The difference, now, is that they are not the only metrics we use to determine our success. We combined McNeal's ideas with our Reveal initiatives and identified the following initial scorecards:

- Mentors—how many Hillcresters were mentoring at Cleveland?
- Reading buddies—how many Cleveland students were being read to (or with) because of Hillcresters? For this one, we used a metric of 10 minutes per child, so if a Hillcrester spent 30 minutes in the school, that counted for three children.
- Adoptions—how many kids had Hillcrest helped to adopt?
- Foster care—how many kids had Hillcresters provided foster care to?

- Backpacks—how many backpacks had Hillcresters sponsored?

We took it a step further as Pastor Doug created signage for each initiative and displayed it throughout the walls of our worship center. Underneath each poster, we had the current number of how we were doing compared to the goal that we had set for that initiative.

Every time a Hillcrester volunteered to be a mentor or a reading buddy, we would change the number.

Every time a Hillcrest family adopted a child, we would change the number. On a Sunday morning, in the middle of the worship service, we'd highlight the family, and they would walk over and change the number.

Whether you were a lifelong Hillcrester or a first-time visitor, it was easy to experience what our church was about. We literally had it on the walls of the worship center. It also served as the best sermon illustration as Pastor Doug would simply point to the walls or highlight one of the posters to remind us what we were about as a church.

To be a church the community would miss is to be a church that measures success different then the way most churches measure success. We knew we needed goals for our initiatives. We knew we needed a way for people to feel like they were contributing to those goals. We also knew we needed a mechanism where people could see how were doing with those goals in a way that was obvious but not obnoxious. The signs on the walls did that for us. People noticed it. It was mentioned often by first-time visitors as a thing they liked about our church. They would comment that they knew what we were about and that our focus was outside of ourselves. It also gave our church, our people, the knowledge that we, collectively as a church, we're making a difference through the Reveal.

Those numbers represented real people.

People we now knew.

People who became part of our families through adoption.

People we were reading to.

People we were mentoring.

People we were feeding.

In addition to the numbers, Hillcrest was recognized for its commitment to the community in numerous ways that made us proud and provided further evidence we were doing the right things:

- Volunteers of America twice nominated us as a Community Partner of Year for the Sioux Falls Spirit of Volunteerism Award
- Cleveland Elementary nominated us for a Mentoring Organization of the Year award sponsored by the School-Based Mentoring Program. For both this award and prior awards, it was humbling and satisfying to be nominated along with major banks, health systems, and large employers.
- Two Hillcresters, Pastor Doug and Darwin Gramstad, were nominated and received Mentor of the Year awards!
- A Congressional Angel in Adoption Award—Hillcrest was recognized as a Congressional Angel in Adoption in 2008. This award recognized our efforts in helping our families with the financial costs of adoption. It was again a humbling and proud award to be recognized with companies, non-profits, and families who have done so much in the work of adoption.
- In 2013, South Dakota Voices for Children recognized Hillcrest as a Champion for Children for our work with adoption, foster care, and Cleveland.

Perhaps the most satisfying achievements were the awards and distinctions Cleveland received during our partnership time. In the second year of our partnership with Cleveland, Jackie was recognized as a National Distinguished Principal—essentially being named South Dakota's principal of the year!

Also, that year Cleveland Elementary made Adequate Yearly Progress, or AYP in education lingo, for the first (and only) time in the school's history! It was remarkable to watch the joy and celebration when the staff received this news during the back-to-school staff lunch provided by Hillcrest. It would be arrogant to think Hillcrest's involvement was directly responsible for making AYP. Our involvement was more correlation (if even that) then it was causation. It was, though, evidence our partnership was proven as a benefit to both the school and the church.

Two years ago, Gretchen Johnson, Cleveland's gym teacher, was named Sioux Falls' Teacher of the Year! In fact, that year two Cleveland teachers were finalists for this prestigious award. When Gretchen won the award, we celebrated with a school-wide pizza party—sending 92 pizzas (1,104 slices!) over to Cleveland to help them celebrate Gretchen's incredible achievement.

Should We Even Measure Success?

Having shared these achievements, it can be paradoxical with the previous chapter about this work being messy. We like to categorize programs and initiatives into 'either or.'

Either our winter clothing drive was a success *or* it was a failure.

Initiatives such as these, though, require 'both and' thinking.

Our winter clothing drive was *both* messy *and* successful.

It can also seem too business-like to measure success.

Some well-meaning Christians argue that we should do what God calls us to and leave the results up to him. These same well-meaning Christians are the ones, who after a youth ministry spent hundreds or thousands of dollars on an outreach event only to see one student come to Christ, exclaim, "Well, it was worth it for that one student." Yes, of course it was, but I can't help thinking we could have saved the student over a coke at Burger King and saved precious dollars and volunteer hours!

If a church is going to enter into a partnership with a school, it's imperative to set some goals—to be able to know if what you're doing is making a difference by checking numbers and curating stories.

If you are, even if there's some muddiness mixed in, then keep on keeping on.

If you're not, it's not un-Christian to step back and ask why.

Visit with the school's leadership.

Survey your people.

Ask yourself how committed you are to this partnership.

Do these and other gut-check exercises to determine if you and your church are serious about this kind of ministry or if there are motives in play.

Because I'll be honest, I had an ulterior motive in play.

Chapter 10: Growing in Influence

Mentoring really has grown my faith. Each week, I pray for us to have God-glorifying conversation, and throughout the week, I pray my mentee will make good decisions. We will continue meeting when she's in high school, and I'm really excited to see what God will do in this relationship.

Aubrey Gilbert, employee at Good Samaritan Lutheran Society

If you or your church are considering partnering with a local school or building some other bridge into the community, know this going in: community outreach is not a church growth strategy.

The scorecards were great.

The awards and the recognitions were awesome.

It was wonderful knowing people were being impacted by our ministry.

It was affirming knowing we too were being impacted through our new relationships and partnerships.

However, I also believed our efforts would translate into more people attending our services on Sunday mornings and more dollars coming in through the weekly offering.

It was not our primary motivation for partnering with Cleveland, nor for the other Reveal initiatives. We did not set out to do this type of ministry so we could grow as a church. We did not see outreach and community service as a growth strategy for our church. We never talked about it once as a leadership or a staff.

But I'd be lying if I said I didn't think our efforts, our outreach, our service would lead to greater success on those traditional church metrics of attendance and giving.

I envisioned the media covering Hillcrest and our feel-good stories

I envisioned these stories capturing the hearts and minds of those seeking to return to church but also wanting to be part of something different, something outside of themselves.

I envisioned Cleveland's staff and students so overwhelmed by our acts of generosity and caring that they would come over to Hillcrest on a Sunday to check us out and see what we were all about.

I envisioned Hillcresters generating such positive word of mouth with their friends, family, coworkers, and neighbors that those within those circles too would come to Hillcrest, like what they saw, and decide to join us.

I envisioned wrong.

While local media did cover us and produced several great stories, those stories did not translate into greater attendance. Our bridges into the community were not built to grow our organization, even though I thought they would as a secondary byproduct. It never happened, at least in the leaps and bounds that I had incorrectly envisioned. It's also inaccurate that no one came to Hillcrest because of the Reveal or because of the bridges we built into the community. The numbers may not have been what I envisioned, but the quality of the people who came to Hillcrest to check us out was further affirmation we were doing the right things as a church. We would also begin to see residual impacts from our community efforts and experience our efforts being noticed by others within the community, leading to even more bridge building and community impact.

Unexpected Influence

What did happen—and what I did not envision—was Hillcrest
having unexpected influence on Cleveland as a result of the trust we
had developed with one another. The first area of unexpected
influence was being the invitation to sit in on certain hiring
committees. It was a unique experience when Jackie called and asked
if I would participate with this team as they met with applicants for
open teaching positions. It was quite the honor to be asked! It was
also a bit weird to be the only person in the room not employed by
the district (it was probably just as weird for the other members on
the team, too!), but it was another opportunity to extend influence
and solidify Hillcrest's partnership with Cleveland.

And let's not overstate my presence on this team or my influence on
the decisions. My involvement wasn't the 'end-all' with these hiring
decisions. We were one step in the process, and this was the only step
I was involved with. We were pre-assigned certain questions to ask,
and there wasn't much time allowed for follow-up questions or
discussion. Jackie took a risk by inviting me to be part of the process,
and looking back, it was a great experience. I also couldn't help but
feel that this—being invited into another level of influence within
Cleveland—while unique and out of the ordinary—was yet another
thing that we, as Hillcrest, could point to when it came to being a
church the community would miss. I mean, how many pastors have
sat in on hiring committees for a local public school?!

A second area of influence came through our formal participation on
Cleveland's Olweus Bully Prevention Committee. Perhaps because I
had not messed up my participation with the hiring team(!), I was
also invited to be part of Cleveland's team that would implement the
Olweus Bully Prevention training that the Sioux Falls School District
was implementing throughout the district. The team consisted of
Jackie, the school counselors and selected teachers. It was again such
a privilege to sit in on two days of training and wrestle with how to
implement this training within the school.

We would discuss students who had been bullied and who were potential bullies.

We would discuss what the training meant for the playground and buses.

We would discuss the best ways to get this training to the rest of the school.

And I'll never forget in the midst of the training one of the teachers finding out that an older sibling of one of her students had committed suicide. It was an obvious blow to both the teacher and the rest of the team, as they dealt with their own grief and wrestled with how to proceed as a school.

One of the best unexpected surprises from our partnership with Cleveland was Jackie and her husband, Todd. Jackie clearly remembers being asked each fall to share at our worship services regarding the relationship between Hillcrest and Cleveland, what the needs were for that current year, and how Hillcrest could best be a partner for that upcoming school year.

Jackie remarks, "One year when I did that, the series at that time was so intriguing to me that I went back the next week—and the next week—and the next week. All of that led to the fact that my husband, Todd, and I both attend and serve at Hillcrest now. One of the statements made at the service that I remember so clearly was this: if Hillcrest fell off the face of the earth tomorrow, would anyone in Sioux Falls even know they were gone? Hillcrest lives this out with the serving and relationship with Cleveland."

We didn't partner with Cleveland in the hopes that the principal and her husband would start to attend the church, be baptized at Hillcrest, and later help me out with a Sunday morning sermon (along with Kristie Schreck, the school's librarian)!

We are trying to be a church that has a positive answer for that question that Jackie heard that morning when she was there to share about Cleveland. I'd love to take the credit for that—to point to Jackie and Todd and hold them up as exhibits of what ministry can look like when churches lean into their communities. But that would be such a disservice to the McNamaras and the God whom we both serve.

God was up to a work within Jackie and Todd.

God was also up to a work within Hillcrest.

We were both faithful to that work, and great things happened and continue to happen.

The Hardest Job

It was evident from my two days spent with this team for the bully prevention training that our school teachers have very difficult jobs. Teaching—like the schools they work at—is another popular arm-chair quarterbacking topic.

There's the 'June, July, August' jokes about teachers said with a 'must be nice' tone.

There's the myth that teachers only work when kids are in the school building.

There's the belief that teachers are overpaid or can simply seek out summer work if they're not content with their wages.

The more time I spend in schools, the more I believe that these comments come from folks who have never spent time in schools. A morning or an afternoon as a field trip volunteer is enough to convince the most cynical of parents (and taxpayers) that whatever a teacher earns, it is not enough!

Saying a teacher has a hard job does not make another job less difficult. If you claim a teacher has a difficult job, it does not make a doctor's job less difficult. There's enough job difficulty to go around. What it does is raise awareness of the difficulty of a profession everyone has an opinion about.

There's the temptation to believe that education, schools, and teaching haven't changed much since when the adults who hold these opinions were kids attending school. Parents often do this with teenagers. A parent will compare stories about peer pressure, temptations, and wanting to fit in and normalize the experience as one that is normal and not that difficult or special. Of course, there is truth to the idea that some things do not change. For teenagers and parents, peer pressure is always going to be a relevant topic. We are naïve, however, if we do not acknowledge the challenges that are unique to our present culture. Yes, both parents 'back in the day' and students today may have peer pressure to drink or do drugs. Today's pressure is intensified and more complicated, with social media and everyone always having a camera and a video camera available at a moment's notice.

The same is true with teaching today. We are naïve to think it's simply teaching a lesson plan on mathematics or giving a spelling test. Teachers today, in addition to being teachers, are also often:

counselors,

mediators,

coaches,

supply providers,

parents,

peace keepers,

pastors,

nurses,

dieticians,

judges,

attorneys,

and detectives—just to name a few.

The very minimal time I spend with teachers in my kids' classrooms and on these teams—in addition to hearing stories first-hand from the teachers in my life—confirm the job's challenges and difficulties. The changes in teaching and the profession's increasing difficulty all highlight a profound partnership opportunity for churches to come alongside a local school and simply ask, "How can we help?"

Beyond Cleveland

Another unexpected source of influence for Hillcrest was partnering with organizations who also were interested in serving the community. The first relationship in this area was with Pastor Laura Borman and Wesley United Methodist Church. Pastor Doug and I were invited to a series of meetings with Pastor Laura and leaders from organizations such as the St. Francis House and the Salvation Army to discuss the possibilities of connecting to further improve the Whittier Neighborhood.

We were at first hesitant. First, Hillcrest was miles away from Wesley. Second, we had much less presence than the other organizations when it came to the Whittier Neighborhood. Third, and perhaps most of all, both Pastor Doug and I had been part of similar groups and efforts with very little fruit. We entered into this meeting with admittedly low expectations.

It soon became evident after the first couple of meetings that while the content was good, the new relationships were better. We quickly learned we had much in common with Pastor Laura and Wesley's ministry. Wesley had been operating its own after-school program for students from a nearby elementary school with similar demographics and needs as Cleveland. They had upwards of 50 or so students in attendance with their program. Since Wesley was an older congregation with much of their congregation on limited and fixed incomes, they were grant-writing (and grant—receiving!) experts. These grants funded their program including the hiring of their own director and offering summer programs.

We soon discovered that one of Wesley's challenges with their after-school program was that it stopped after fifth grade as students moved into middle school at Whittier. Pastor Laura and the church would see some of these students in their midweek programs but lost contact with many of the students once they entered middle school. Wesley desired to do more for these middle school students. They hated seeing them drop off, but their volunteer and financial resources were already stretched with their own booming after-school program.

Enter Hillcrest.

When we partnered with Cleveland, we had a phase two in mind of running an after-school program or center for middle school students in the Whitter Neighborhood. We knew Cleveland fed into Whittier, and it would be natural to consider extending our partnership. We cautiously leaned into this effort, as we didn't want to step on toes or double up on ministry efforts. We were also cautious because the type of ministry we were discussing didn't really exist. There were plenty of after-school options for middle school students throughout Sioux Falls. None of the options offered a holistic approach from a church and director who was living in the community amidst the students.

Early on there were cautions and anxieties. Month after month our leadership would discuss what this project would look like. These conversations were often circular and frustrating! We struggled to wrap our heads around this type of ministry we could not really describe.

There were three obstacles in shaping this ministry to Whittier and the neighborhood:

1. What was the ministry going to do?
2. Where was the ministry going to happen?
3. Who was going to lead the ministry?

The first challenge was what the ministry was going to do. Our staff and leadership had differing ideas on what this ministry was going to look like.

Some thought of it as a traditional after-school program.

Some envisioned a more holistic approach, with Hillcrest having a permanent geographical presence within the community and being able to provide additional ministry opportunities in addition to a more traditional after-school program.

The first challenge—what we were going to do—was made much more difficult because of the second challenge—where this ministry was going to be located.

We pursued running a program out of Wesley's existing building.

We were sitting on a pile of money from our own land sale, so we also thought of buying our own place and converting it into a space for our after-school program. In addition to this idea being expensive (we'd need to buy a house and also renovate it for an after-school program), it too was made much more difficult because of the third challenge—who was going to lead this ministry.

We could get the purpose right and have the right location, but we knew we needed the right person to lead this ministry. Again, we had options.

We looked inward to see if there was a leader within our midst who was called and capable of leading this ministry. Names would come to mind, we'd pray about those names, check in with those names, and those names would pass. We knew this ministry wasn't going to be one we wanted to launch without a leader or to hire someone into. We were building this ministry and wanted to build it with someone. In that way, it was different then our normal ministries, like our children's ministry, where we typically would have posted the position, sought applicants, and hired the best one.

This position was different. This ministry was new and required a certain temperament and skill set. We needed a director who understood after-school programming but also understood the unique challenges and possibilities with ministry being done in the community.

It was a bit of chicken-and-egg discussion for us. We narrowed in on ministry purpose, and still needed a location and a leader.

If we had the leader but didn't have a location, we risked no longer having a leader.

If we had the location but didn't have the leader, we risked wasting resources on a location without any students or leader!

Both those questions would be answered during the 2009–10 school year at about the same time. We shared our sharpened vision with Wesley's leadership, who indicated they had a parsonage on their church property that could be a good fit for our middle school after-school program. It had been years since Wesley's pastor lived in the parsonage. Wesley rented it out and used the income to assist with its budget. The condition of the house was rough, so Wesley wasn't going to be able to continue to rent out the house without making some significant repairs and updates. They didn't have the money for such repairs, and so their ability to utilize the house for income was not a long-term solution.

For Hillcrest, the idea of the running the ministry from this house provided two main benefits. The most obvious was being on Wesley's property. It wasn't rocket science to make an assumption that kids who had gone to Wesley's after-school program would have an easier transition to this location. Instead of heading to Wesley after school, they would walk across the parking lot and go to the house after school. The second was while the home needed significant repairs, the structure and foundation were good. It was going to be an expensive remodel, but still more cost-effective then buying a different property and having to renovate it.

With a viable lead on a location, we turned to leadership. It just so happened that Jessi Matson, our missionary to inner-city Detroit, was hearing God's whispers to return home but to remain engaged in similar ministry. We reached out to her, and she indicated substantial interest and calling to return home and help up launch this program. There were many, many hoops to go through before this ministry had actual students coming to it, but we had answered our three main challenges: purpose, place, and person.

What followed narrowing down our purpose, place, and person was a whole lot of work.

We held demolition weekends in May that year to gut the basement, tear down walls, and demo much of the upstairs.

We met with an architect for a design of the basement where the program would be held.

We took the architect's plans to city hall to make sure we we're good to go from a code perspective and to attain a building permit.

We went to city planning to apply for a conditional use permit so we could operate what the city would call a day care in a residential section. I attended the city council meeting just in case there were questions on our permit and was relieved when there were none!

We partnered with a contractor in our church to oversee the project and keep the various subcontractors moving. The house would require a new furnace, air conditioner, new plumbing throughout the basement, and new electrical throughout the house, in addition to some internal framing changes and wall reconfigurations.

While the house was busy being readied for kids to come that August, I set about to secure outside funds to help run the Powerhouse. Hillcrest had budgeted monies to operate the program, but as we were brand new with this kind of ministry, we didn't really grasp what it would cost to run it. I researched grant options that fit our mission and organization and sent grant applications to over 20 local and national foundations. Like much in life, it only takes one, and our one successful application was approved by the Sioux Falls Area Community Foundation, who awarded the Powerhouse a $7,500 grant to be given over a three-year period in equal amounts.

It's easy to say that the grant from the Sioux Falls Area Community Foundation felt like further confirmation that we were doing what we were supposed to be doing. I can't say for sure how or if the program would have been different without the grant, except that it would have cost us more money! It felt like validation to have a group outside of us believe in us enough to make a financial contribution. It also gave us credibility when explaining the ministry to potential students, families, and even Whittier.

Jessi would settle into the home that summer, even while construction was still going on, and while things were not perfect, we were ready to go by the first day of school in August of 2010. We learned so much that first year and in the years to come. Jessi was an absolutely perfect fit for Powerhouse, the students, and the location. Her experience with City Mission and Detroit's Brightmoor District were perfect for leading Powerhouse. Having lived in inner-city Detroit, it was going to take a lot to rattle Jessi, though there were times her experience in the Whittier Neighborhood rivaled that of

Detroit. Jessi's heart for people—the students and their families—won them over to her in no time.

Research told us that middle school students who passed and did well in English and math had higher high school graduation rates than their peers who did not do so well. We tailored our program—and the grant that we were awarded—to insuring that our students were proficient and excelling at math and language arts. As anyone with a middle school student knows far too well, though, it can be rather challenging to get a middle school student to do homework, study for a test, or finish a project right after school. They're hungry, they've been to school all day, and they'd much rather do just about anything then more school work. Jessi knew this and adapted the program to meet both relational and academic objectives. She balanced the program's relational aspects with its academics, making sure students were proficient and passing their math and language arts classes, while also insuring they had fun at the same time.

Hillcrest provided 1–2 volunteers each day to work with Jessi and the students. Powerhouse was another opportunity for Hillcresters to experience and participate in the Reveal with their hands and feet. They were working closely with under-resourced kids, establishing consistent relationships, and assisting students to succeed personally and academically.

As with any work or ministry, especially one involving middle school students, there were good days and not-so-good days. There were times when students would pass a big test or confide with Jessi or a volunteer about a problem at home, and Jessi would be able to speak into that situation. There were the various field trips to the Country Apple Orchard, Downtown Sioux Falls, the Empire Mall, and the waterpark at the Brandon Holiday Inn Express that provided experiences that many middle-class students and families take for granted.

The not-so-good days included the Powerhouse being broken into and being vandalized, volunteers being mistreated, and students who at times did not care about school or other responsibilities. It was eye-opening for many of us to experience this reality of ministry in a more urban context. It was challenging to experience that not everyone was thrilled or excited about our presence. It was faith-stretching to discuss what to do when a window was broken or when the house was broken into or when something was stolen.

We were pretty green when it came to these more challenging issues and learned by trial and error. We wanted to err on the side of the student and yet not get taken advantage of. We want to err on the side of grace and yet not lose volunteers who (understandably) had a more black-and-white perspective. As I would meet weekly with Jessi and personally check in often on the Powerhouse, I would hear and see the tension at work. Thankfully, Jessi had experience with the tension from her time in Detroit. She already knew what we did not—that this kind of ministry is messy. That this kind of ministry is accompanied by ups as well as downs. That this kind of ministry can be difficult for those who are expecting to see quick turnarounds or easy fixes. That this kind of ministry can be hard for those who are used to operating with a middle-class mindset.

Chapter 11: Stopping and Starting

I continue to be amazed at the passion, dedication, and selflessness that Hillcrest shares and shows with us. When adults are lifted up here, it translates directly to our students, creating that positive and productive learning environment for all.

Mitch Schaefer, current Cleveland Elementary principal

We operated Powerhouse for six school years. At the height of the program, over 20 students attended Powerhouse on any given day. After six years, we made the difficult decision to close Powerhouse. Our director had resigned to focus on other things and our numbers had dwindled down to about 2–4 students. Changes in Wesley's after-school program affected their abilities to 'feed' students into Powerhouse. In addition to the low numbers, we also could not identify a leader who could take over and bring the program back to its earlier heyday.

In 15 years of ministry, I've found the decision to end a ministry or a program is difficult and emotional. There's plenty of good reasons for why these decisions are particularly painful. In most cases, the program or ministry was started to meet a real need—to accomplish real ministry. Churches can be guilty of over-programming, but it's rare a program or ministry wasn't started to meet some need. Needs get met, relationships get developed, and schedules adapt to make the program or ministry a part of the church member or family's schedule. Add to that the velocity of change happening elsewhere in people's lives and the subtle and unspoken belief that the church should be the one place where people are safe from the changes they encounter on a seemingly daily basis, and you get a perfect storm of sorts for why changes—and closing programs—is met with spirited resistance.

We've closed many popular programs and ministries in my time at Hillcrest, and none was ever easy or fun. I closed down the enormously popular AWANA program and can still show you those battle wounds! The decision to close a ministry is similar to the criteria we use when deciding whether to start a new ministry: purpose, leadership, and resources. In the case of AWANA, the purpose was always clear—a fun program for children to memorize scripture and grow in their love for God. No problem with the purpose.

The program's leadership was another story. We had difficulty in finding consistent leadership for AWANA. Of the many hats I've worn at Hillcrest, AWANA Commander is perhaps the most surprising. I led the program for a year while we decided what we were going to do. No one wanted to step up to lead it, even those who had a deep support for AWANA. It doesn't matter if it's Sunday school, worship team, or youth ministry, it's nearly impossible to pull it off without leadership.

The final factor was a resource factor. AWANA was a historically expensive ministry and utilized most of the building on Wednesday nights. This often meant allocating our youth ministry a less-than-ideal time to meet if they wanted to use the gym for their program. We recognized our children's ministries already had the use of the gym at the other prime time for a church—Sunday mornings—and here on Wednesday evenings they again had the prime time for use of the gym.

These factors led us to close AWANA, shift to our own invented kids' midweek program, and eventually pave the way for Wednesday Night Service. It gave our student ministries Wednesday nights back for use of the gym. It's clear there would have been no Wednesday Night Service without the closing of AWANA.

Can't Do Everything

It can feel like failure when you stop a program or ministry. When we closed Powerhouse, we admitted we could no longer do this ministry and this ministry was not worth the resources we were pouring into it. It's hard not to feel that sense of failure.

Like we quit.

Like we weren't good enough to keep it going.

Another lesson we learned the hard way is that we can't be all things to everyone, even if those things are really good community ministry opportunities that appear to be a perfect fit with our mission.

Safe Families was one such ministry.

Safe Families was a nationwide initiative aimed at providing children a safe home as an alternative to entering the foster care system. It's a brilliant concept and idea. There are lots of children who would benefit from time in a different home due to unforeseen circumstances.

Their only parent loses a job.

Their only parent is hospitalized for a long period of time.

Without any friends or family to take these children in, the only real alternative is foster care, an already overloaded system in many places throughout the country.

The program began in Chicago with great success, and soon other cities were employing it to help their overcrowded foster care systems. Bethany Christian Services, whom we partnered with for several adoptions, was hosting the program for Sioux Falls. Hillcrest was a natural ask for joining this program on the ground floor and seeing it take off throughout Sioux Falls. We met with Bethany's leadership, pitched the idea to our leadership council, and agreed to be a partnering church for Safe Families. This meant promoting the ministry and providing families to become safe families. We were on the initial leadership team for Safe Families, where I met with point leaders from other churches who were also implementing safe families to share best practices, promote the ministry, and encourage one another.

Hillcrest launched the ministry similar to our other ministry partnerships. We introduced the leadership at Sunday morning services, heard their story and passion, and invited Hillcresters to partner with Safe Families. The uniqueness of the pitch for Hillcrest was that we already had adoption and foster care firmly part of our culture. Safe Families was ideal for people who felt the nudge for adoption or foster care, but for whatever reason, it wasn't the right time to jump into those commitments. Safe Families provided similar ministry with a beginning and a (theoretical) ending point. It was theoretical because the nationwide average for a child staying in a Safe Family was six weeks (although Sioux Falls' experience was going to be about six months!).

In addition to being a safe family, there were two additional ways to get involved with the ministry:

- You could provide resources for families in Safe Families, such as a crib for a family taking in an infant but whose own baby days were long gone. Several Hillcresters provided resources, and Susan, a Hillcrester, oversaw the donations made to Safe Families and housed the items in her garage.
- You could be a Safe Family coach, whose responsibility was to serve as a liaison between the Safe Family and the family whose child or children were in the care of the Safe Family. The coach would serve as a mentor for the family and also as a support system for the Safe Family, insuring that they had everything they needed and weren't being ignored once there was a placement. One Hillcrester served as a coach for over a year.

What we had a difficult time with was in the provision of Safe Families.

There was some interest, but the interest waned with the completing of the online application or the necessary training needed to become a Safe Family. I became increasingly uncomfortable at our leadership meetings as the other churches had seemingly no problem in raising up Safe Families, while Hillcrest would not have a single trained Safe Family in over two years of promoting the ministry. Rather than renew our commitment for a third year, we decided Hillcrest's efforts and resources would best be spent elsewhere, and we ended our formal relationship with Safe Families.

On the outside looking in, this was another failure.

What is unique about Hillcrest, though, is that in the time we were officially on board with Safe Families, we were continuing our partnership with Cleveland along with the other Reveal initiatives. Our failure with Safe Families led us to make the difficult decision that Hillcrest couldn't be involved in every great ministry or program that would come through our city. We had to double down on the efforts we were already good at, that we were already seeing success with. If God meant for us to be with Safe Families, God would have risen up those Safe Families. I realize as I say it that it's possible to use that as an excuse.

Not at all.

We tried.

We really did.

We got the word out.

We recruited.

We invited.

We promoted.

We shared vision.

For whatever reason, God said, "Not this one."

The decisions to close the Powerhouse and no longer be a Safe Families church were hard. They weren't easy.

It does make me smile, though, when I realize what God is able to do with our faithfulness with those hard decisions. Those decisions freed up resources and energies for:

- Cleveland Playground Fundraising Assistance—Hillcrest's annual craft fair—one of our biggest annual fundraisers used to support Powerhouse's operating costs. Once the Powerhouse closed, we needed a new partner to support with the craft fair funds. It just so happened that Cleveland was in the middle of raising funds for new playground equipment. We designated Cleveland to receive the craft fair funds and further our partnership in a unique way.
- Orphan Care Ministry—our Reveal monies will not last forever. Our leadership team and our orphan care ministry team had already discussed ways to continue this ministry once those funds were gone, but we were very much still in 'what if' mode. Our closure of the Powerhouse enabled us to budget funds in our operating budget for the continuation of our adoption ministry for the foreseeable future.
- Sending a new missionary from Hillcrest—we were able to significantly sponsor the sending of Brianna Lietha as a Youth For Christ missionary to Germany! If we continued to be a Safe Families Church and operating the Powerhouse, our support of Brianna would have been nominal—similar to the other organizations we support. One can say it is coincidental that our timing to free up significant resources by closing the Powerhouse just so

happened to line up with Brianna's call to missions. Or one can say God used one to accomplish the other.

I admit that I tend to roll my eyes at Christian clichés such as "when God closes a door, he opens a window." The theology breaks down as soon as you're in the midst of a health crisis or are caring for a friend who's undergoing cancer or a painful divorce. The cliché—the theology—doesn't always hold up.

I believe wholeheartedly in seizing on opportunities God presents you. It can be you as an individual, you as your family, or you as your organization. Our experience has been that in order to seize certain opportunities, we need to let go of other ones. In order to be open to new efforts and ministries, sometimes you need to close down other ones. I don't see these decisions as ones where you can make the potentially wrong choice. I don't see these decisions where if you choose A (keeping up with Safe Families), then you're sinning and bad things will happen whereas if you choose B (closing Safe Families and doubling down on adoptions), then you've made the correct choice and thus God will bless you. I grew up on *Choose Your Own Adventure* books, and it's easy to take this kind of thinking into both our personal and corporate relationship with God.

That if we make one choice—and it's not the correct choice—then somehow we've displeased God and will suffer for it.

Are there decisions like that in life? Decisions where one is sinful and one is not? Certainly!

I just don't believe that the decisions about this ministry or that program fall into that category. I believe God could have honored, used, and redeemed either potential decision. There is no denying, though, that the commitment to Powerhouse and Safe Families would have been, in classical economics terminology, an opportunity cost for us. It's possible we could have seen some fruit by staying the course with either ministry.

It's known, though, that had we stayed the course with those programs, we would have missed out on current opportunities.

Changes in Leadership

After a few years at Cleveland, Jackie McNamara resigned to be the principal of the school in her hometown. While we certainly understood the decision, and saw more of Jackie since she was attending Hillcrest, we were also sad, knowing that the trust and relationship we had developed was unique and not easily reproducible. The new principal came to Cleveland from leading an elementary on Sioux Falls' west side. The only similarity between both schools was that both had large enrollments. At that back-to-school lunch that we provided for Cleveland each August, we met Anne Burchill Williams and shared things we had done in the past and what we could do in the future. Anne jokingly inquired about coming to Hillcrest on Sundays as a prerequisite for our partnership. We of course said no! We were happy to help in whatever ways we could.

If making a good first impression is important when starting out a partnership, it is just as important when partnering with an organization going through transition. One of Cleveland's first-grade teachers desired some writing curriculum that would help her teaching and benefit students. Gretchen, the gym teacher, inquired about gym shoes for students she knew would be showing up to school without them next week. We quickly said yes to both requests because they were both good requests, but we also wanted to demonstrate to Anne the kind of partner we could be for the Cleveland community.

As of this writing, Anne will be moving to another school and we'll be partnering with our third principal in 10 years. The principal is Mitch Schaefer, whom I quoted to start this chapter. Mitch was Jackie McNamara's assistant principal when we first partnered with Cleveland, so it's a 'full circle' moment for all of us, and for Hillcrest, it will be another opportunity to demonstrate the level of commitment and passion Hillcrest has for serving this local school right in her backyard.

BRIAN STROH

Epilogue

Whether it was our work with Cleveland, the Powerhouse, Genesis, or Safe Families, as a church we were exposed to parts of our city and community that are easy to overlook. All of us had functioned just fine without getting involved with these initiatives. We perhaps knew there was some poverty within our city when we saw the homeless guy begging for money at an off-ramp or when we made our annual trip to The Banquet and served supper and interacted with people much different than us. But it was easy for us to forget those experiences, or even worse, pat ourselves on our proverbial backs because we served for an evening or gave a beggar some loose change and then went back to our normal lives without any real heart change. For the most part, you can live, work, and play in our community without ever having to confront the reality that many in our city experience day to day.

In our city, the idea of churches partnering with schools has caught on. Trinity Baptist works with Garfield Elementary. Oak Hills partners with Hawthorne. Celebrate works with Terry Redlin. All of these are elementary schools with similar demographics as Cleveland. Pastor Doug and I recently met with leaders from Our Savior's Lutheran who are looking to partner with a local school. The idea has certainly caught on, not just in Sioux Falls but throughout the country, as churches look for meaningful ways to serve their neighbors and communities.

Education has been a big value for my life as long as I can remember. When I was about to head to kindergarten, my grandparents—my mom's parents—took me school supply shopping. I didn't understand the significance of this moment at the time, but as I grew older my mom would tell me how much her dad valued education, and even though he was only able to complete the eighth grade before going to work on the family farm, he still greatly valued

113

education, passing that value onto his four daughters. He and Grandma taking me school supply shopping would be a ritual that would continue with the other grandchildren.

My mom worked as a teacher for 40 years and, along with my dad, continued to impress the value of education on to me and my siblings. Each of us siblings remembers being paid to read books during the summer. I don't remember the exact amount, but I do know it spurred on a love for reading that continues to this day. I'm sure some will challenge or roll their eyes at paying their kids to read—I can understand the sentiment.

We desire for kids to be intrinsically motivated to read.

We know that kids who are motivated by an extrinsic reward—be it money or a Pizza Hut Book-It coupon—might struggle with the habit of reading once the reward is removed.

No money or pizza—no reading. The counterargument then is to figure how to get kids reading without the extrinsic reward, without the payoff.

But here's the thing: many of us in today's economy are paid to read. I don't mean that we are literally paid to sit in an office and read a book.

But we are paid to read.

The following quote has been attributed to many, including Charlie Jones and John Wooden: "In 5 years you'll be the same person you are today except for the people you meet and the books you read."

Meaning if you want to grow as a person, grow as a leader, grow in your profession or job, you need to be a reader. Your company or organization isn't going to necessarily pay you a bonus or a stipend for you to read. But if you continue to read and grow in your work performance and competency as a result of your reading, it's highly likely you'll be making more then you did prior to the reading and the growth in performance and output.

Too Busy to Read

The "I don't have time to read" is a frequent excuse given by both students and adults.

I don't sit at my office and read a book, except on those occasions when it comes to sermon preparation. My reading is done outside of my official office time. I read in the morning before work or in the evening before going to bed. Most of us have no problem making time for a movie or our favorite television shows. I'm convinced that television is the enemy of most any productive effort in our lives. I frequently tell my own kids that the goal of life isn't to watch as much television as you can. During the school year, if I find one of them watching a show instead of studying for a test or quiz, I'll make the passive-aggressive comment of wondering if what he or she is watching is going to be on tomorrow's exam. In the summer time, Tarina and I insist that each child reads for part of the day—in addition to other activities including a workout or athletic practice, musical instrument practice, and household chores—before the television or other screens are turned on.

I'm sure I border on grouch or strict or out of touch when it comes to this part of my psyche. When one of my children was asked by a teacher what he was going to do this summer, he listed off some activities and also mentioned that he would have to read some books because his parents (us!) would make him.

I'm not anti-television or screens. I can waste time on Twitter with the best of them.

But our devices, our screens, our shows and our social media are robbing us of the opportunity to better our lives. Bernadette Jiwa writes the following in her book *Hunch: Turn Your Everyday Insights Into the Next Big Thing*:

"Most of us check our phones within 5 minutes of waking and go on to check them an average of 46 times per day. That number is rising and it's significantly higher for younger demographics. Some research suggests that some people check their phones up to 150 times a day. We're spending most of our waking hours reacting and responding to external inputs that we allow to steal our attention—those important, non-urgent, emails and notifications that draw us in. We've stopped taking time to notice and to question, to think and to reflect and to just be. And our lives and the quality of our ideas and our work are poorer for it."

(p. 34)

We make time for the things, the activities and the people that are important to us.

When it comes to whether to read a book or watch a show, we make time for what is most important to us.

And when it comes to partnering with an under-resourced school or continuing on with ministry as normal, we make time for what is important for us.

It will take time.

It will take effort.

It will take an 'in it for the long haul' attitude.

But it's worth it.

It's incredibly worth it.

Acknowledgements

There are many people to acknowledge and thank for making this book a reality:

- Hillcrest Church for the sabbatical and the subsequent time granted for this project and also for taking a risk on the idea of partnering with a public school over 10 years ago when it was crazy and no one was doing it

- Hillcrest's elders and staff for the support given throughout the project and for being the book's first readers

- Pastor Doug Bartel for his belief in this project and his leadership in connecting other churches with public schools

- Jackie McNamara for risking on a sight unseen partnership with a church she had never heard of and pastors she didn't know. I'm also grateful for her endorsement of the book

- Cleveland's teachers and staff for their gracious accommodation of our church to be their business partner.

- Sheri Levisay for editing the book. Her insights and comments were priceless and made this a better read for you!

- Sam Otis for the front and back cover design His professional craftmanship helped make this look and feel like a book

- My Friday morning men's group for continuing to ask about the book and encouraging its completion

- MK, Tom and Trevor for their gracious book endorsements

- The Dachtlers for their continual love and support during the process, publishing recommendations and contacts, and potential outlets for the published book

- The Strohs for their continual love and support during the process and for an incredible childhood to witness the high value placed on education and public school teachers

- Riley, Wesley, Charley and Kinsley for putting up with dad during the ups and downs of this journey and for flourishing as young people living the story found in this book

- Finally for Tarina for her amazing love and support for this project. There were many times where I wanted to quit or let the project die and her faith and encouragement saw this to completion. This is our story and our journey and I am incredibly grateful to be on it with you!

Appendix A

50 ways a church can partner with a school

1. Pray for students and staff—it seems clichéd to start the list this way, but there's power in a church praying for a school. Because of our developed trust with Cleveland, we've been invited to pray when students have passed away, when there's been conflict within the school, and when there's been hardship or crises within the school or within families who attend the school.
2. Sponsor the back-to-school staff meal—this is an easy win for churches. Whether you cook it yourselves or cater it in, the results are the same!
3. Provide a meal at fall conferences—another easy win, and helps an under-resourced school's PTA stretch a tight budget.
4. Provide a meal at spring conferences—see #3.
5. Buy a box of Kleenex for every classroom.
6. Buy a bottle of hand sanitizer for every classroom.
7. Buy a thing of Clorox wipes for every classroom.
8. Do #5–7 at least twice a year.
9. Buy the teacher lounge a Keurig.
10. Stock the teacher lounge with plenty of K-cups.
11. Ask the teachers for a wish list for their classrooms and then get those items. We've bought shoes, Post-it notes, highlighters, and other items teachers need.
12. Provide an inflatable obstacle course for the last day of school.
13. Provide freeze pops for the last day of school.
14. Be a mentor.
15. Be a reading buddy.
16. Volunteer with an after-school activity like Girls on the Run.
17. Volunteer at the book fair.

18. Volunteer on picture day.
19. Volunteer for a field trip.
20. Make a business card with your staff person's contact information so teachers and staff can contact you directly with needs they have.
21. Vote in local school board elections.
22. Use social media to highlight good things happening at your school.
23. Donate physical resources you no longer use with your school.
24. Allow your school's PTA to use your parking lot for a car wash.
25. Give the librarian Amazon or Barnes & Noble gift cards to stock the library with current titles.
26. Buy a book for every teacher at the book fair off his or her wish list.
27. Write encouragement cards for teachers and staff—ask the school for a staff list and write out encouragement cards for the staff to let them know you're praying for them, that they're doing a great job, to keep it up. While anytime can be a good time for these types of cards, back to school, the holidays, and toward the end of the school year are naturally good times for this type of gesture.
28. Put in a small gift card with those encouragement cards—this requires some funds, but many teachers don't receive the gifts and the appreciation that their peers do in other school environments. Of course, they're not in it for the appreciation or the gift, but teachers are human beings, and every one of us wants to be appreciated and recognized. When doing this, make sure to include the whole staff!
29. Free a staff member to devote 'office' time to the school— Hillcrest has been so generous in allowing me time during the week to spend on the school, whether it's setting up a meal, reading with a student, or organizing a winter supply drive. The more serious your intentions with the school, the more necessary it will be for someone on staff to be able to devote some work time to the partnership.

30. Allow the school to utilize your building—we're rookies in this suggestion, but several churches allow their building to be used by school for fine arts concerts and performances as well as an off-site meeting area for teachers and staff. The bulk of our church facilities sit vacant for too much of the week. Churches have all kinds of opportunities to steward their facilities to serve schools and the community.

31. Help the school care about its facility and property—janitorial and custodial personnel are often stretched thin at schools, doing all they can to simply clean the building each and every day. Churches can provide volunteers to tackle projects the school can't get to including basic landscaping and removing unwanted language off of playground equipment.

32. Volunteer to wipe down desks and other sanitize the tops of desks and other common areas during cold and flu season.

33. Invite school leaders to share with your church—few people in a community know how things are actually going in a community better than a school teacher or a principal. Inviting them to share with you in a worship context validates experience and opens your church to a wealth of insight and perspective.

34. Allow the school to serve you—most relationships work best when both sides are giving and receiving. The school you're serving will most likely want to give back to you and your church. Make this possible. Cleveland's staff has donated candy for our Trunk or Treat event, provided Hillcresters with free tickets to their annual pancake supper, and allowed our youth ministry to use gym equipment as a demonstration of appreciation.

35. Network to meet other needs—the soccer goals at Cleveland didn't have nets for the longest time. One of our members works at Dakota Alliance and got nets donated for the playground. Early in our partnership Jackie noticed a need for haircuts for several students. One of our members is a very popular stylist and came in once a week to cut hair! Depending on the need, there's going to be some 'red tape'

involved, but once you've established trust, the time to get through the red tape is significantly lowered.

36. Celebrate wins with your school—help your school celebrate when students win by making Annual Yearly Progress goals or having one of the staff or teachers recognized. There's often little funding available for the school to do much celebrating, and helping the school celebrate can boost morale for the entire school.

37. Empower church members to meet needs—the more involved your church gets within a school, the more opportunities there will be to demonstrate care. Many of these will bubble up from those church members who are volunteering or working within the school. A coat for a second-grader. Gym shoes for a third-grader. Personal hygiene items for fifth-graders. Budget funds your church members can access to meet these needs when they come across them.

38. Take the principal to coffee and listen to his or her heart.

39. Donate to DonorsChoose.org projects from your school's teachers and classrooms.

40. Coach a recreational team from your school.

41. Allow sports teams from your school to use your gym for practices.

42. Send flowers to teachers on the first day of the year.

43. Bring the front office staff coffee.

44. Host an after-school program for students from your school.

45. Provide or sponsor a summer readiness camp for incoming kindergarten students.

46. Buy curriculum for teachers.

47. Have your pastor or other church leaders participate in reading weeks and read to classrooms.

48. Pick up the tab for mentors' lunches who mentor at your school.

49. Work with the other non-profits who benefit your school including feeding organizations.

50. Dream big with the school—we've already discussed the computers we purchased for the school, but it's this type of

thing that qualifies as dreaming big with the school. Who knows what may come from such outlandish dreaming? Perhaps you can't add on space to the school, but you can provide items or tools—like a mobile computer lab—that better utilize already existing space.

Appendix B

Original Proposal to Hillcrest Leadership

Overview

Hillcrest has recently been challenged with two key questions:

- Are the people in my life (coworkers, relatives, neighbors, etc.) better off because of my relationship with Jesus?
- Would Sioux Falls protest if Hillcrest were to cease existence as a church?

An honest assessment, at least to the second question, would be "probably not," hence the strong emphasis on Sunday morning teaching and Council meetings on building bridges into the community. In examining and reflecting on what God seems to be doing in Hillcrest's life (and also in my own life and my family's life) is a pull into the local community, particularly the east side of Sioux Falls.

I live less than a mile away from Hillcrest and less than two blocks away from Cleveland Elementary School. I live on a block with several (at least seven) homes with elementary-aged children and have come to learn that only one kid attends Cleveland, though it is by far the closest school. The perception is that Cleveland is a substandard school, with many families that have the means and ability opting for other educational options: either open-enroll to other (more perceived better) school, enroll their children in private school, or homeschool their children. My family and I are already making the commitment to support Cleveland by sending our boys there and getting involved in whatever ways we can. After looking at some of the data and visiting with Cleveland's principals, I believe there are some strategic projects out there for a church like Hillcrest looking to build a bridge into the community.

A Geographical Reason

One reason that Cleveland presents a strategic importance is the number of Hillcresters who live in its district. Hillcresters with school-aged children, while spread throughout 19 Sioux Falls' Elementary schools, cluster in three east-side elementary school districts:

- Cleveland—20 Hillcrest Families, or roughly 20% (1 out of 5) Hillcrest families with school-aged children live in this district
- John Harris—17 Hillcrest families, or 17%
- Harvey Dunn—14 Hillcrest families, or 15%

When you include Hillcresters without school-aged children, the spread grows to 24 different elementary school districts, but the clustering still takes place in predominantly east-side elementary school districts:

- Cleveland—31 Hillcrest Families, or roughly 15% of Hillcrest families with school-aged children live in this district (the highest concentration of Hillcresters within a single district)
- John Harris—30 Hillcrest families, or 14%
- Harvey Dunn—17 Hillcrest families, or 8%

Cleveland is also the second-closest school to Hillcrest, 1.03 miles away, behind only Harvey Dunn (.7 miles) in terms of proximity. When Rosa Parks opens, this will change, but still, the school district with the most Hillcrest families and most Hillcresters is also one of the closest geographically to Hillcrest.

An Educational Reason

Cleveland is a Title I School, meaning its "No Child Left Behind" scores are less than the suggested benchmarks. A snapshot at some of Cleveland's educational statistics:

- 109 Cleveland students have a diagnosed disability, or roughly 20% of the school; rank of sixth-highest disability numbers among Sioux Falls schools
- 111 Cleveland students are classified as ESL (English as a Second Language), rank of second-highest among Sioux Falls schools
- Cleveland has a 40+ page document on goals and objectives related to increasing educational performance; an obvious need to increase scores in reading, math, and composition

Hillcrest has at least 15 certified teachers who could assist, lead, and coach our community on things like how to be mentors, how to read to kids, how to help kids with homework, as well as offer on-site or off-site opportunities for kids to increase their academic skills (like this summer's "East Side Kindercamp")

An Economic Reason

Almost half (48.4%) of Cleveland students are either on free or reduced meals. Several students come from homes where it is difficult to make ends meet. Things like money for school lunches, holiday parties, school supplies, or winter clothing are hard to come by for roughly 1 out of every 2 kids at Cleveland school.

Cleveland is also one of the more diverse schools in the Sioux Falls District; 74% of its students white, and the other 25% divided (in descending order of concentration): black, Hispanic, Native American, and Asian. This is a relatively close mission field in which we would have the opportunity to close the gap between those who have and those who don't, especially children who typically are victims of situations outside of their control.

A Strategic Reason

I met with both of Cleveland's principals on May 29 to discover what
needs they might have and how Hillcrest could potentially assist
those efforts. I communicated that we were not looking to set up an
after-school Bible club or looking to run our propaganda through
their organization; that we were simply interested in meeting needs.
We talked about resource needs, facility needs, and financial needs.
The principals shared some exciting opportunities that exist to
Hillcrest. The main needs they identified are the following:

- Reading buddies—These are adults who would listen to kids
  reading out loud—research shows kids that read out loud
  retain more and increase comprehension and thus do better
  on standardized testing.
- Mentor families—Cleveland has a high number of refugee
  family students. This initiative would partner a refugee family
  with an American family that is settled into the culture and
  could help navigate these families through the system.
- Mentoring program—this is a two-fold opportunity. First,
  mentor adults would simply desire to have a positive
  influences on kids, through weekly meetings, lunches at the
  school, etc. Second, no such program exists at Cleveland, and
  there may be opportunity to assist with starting the program.
- Clothing drives—there is a high need for winter clothes for
  many of Cleveland's families (coats, boots, socks, underwear;
  families underestimate how cold it can actually get). The
  potential would also exist for school supply drives in the fall
  before school starts.
- Parenting skills—there is also a need for basic parenting skills
  and tips (consistent bedtimes, not arguing with people in
  front of kids, etc.).

These are the needs that the principals shared. There is currently no
other church or non-profit group working strategically with
Cleveland, so there wouldn't be any 'turf' issues, though it would
allow for an exciting opportunity to partner with the many churches

that are close to Cleveland with this endeavor.

Some other ways we could come alongside Cleveland:

- Back to school appreciation—donating gift cards for classroom supplies to Cleveland's teachers, preparing or providing lunch for back-to-school work days, etc.
- Facility needs—the principals weren't sure on facility needs, but we could offer to help new teachers move into classrooms, help teachers set up their rooms on work days, etc.

A SWOT Analysis

Strengths

- High number of certified teachers in Hillcrest
- Geographic and community presence
- Resources and volunteers looking for a bridge building opportunity

Weaknesses

- First project of kind
- Potentially limited finances
- Open enrollment mentality among Hillcrester families

Opportunities

- No one else is doing anything
- Several churches within walking distance to Cleveland, opportunity to partner with other denominations
- An open and welcoming school leadership

Threats

- Highly diversified culture—language and other cultural barriers
- Time—this isn't a quick fix and discouragement may set in
- Other churches may not be apt to jump on board

A Potential Timeline

Upon Leadership Council's discussion, along with suggestion and changes to the proposal, we would move to implement some basic steps through the following timeline:

- LC Discussion
- Follow-up meeting with principals regarding plan, working through many of the following logistics
- Design communication strategy for church (sermons, announcements, etc.)
- Designing goals or targets for this project (# of volunteers, etc.)

Appendix C

Recommended Reading

The Jonathan Effect: Helping Kids and Schools Win the Battle Against Poverty, Mike Tenbusch, 2016

Real Hope in Chicago, Wayne L. Gordon and John Perkins, 1995

Kingdom Calling: Vocational Stewardship for the Common Good, Amy L. Sherman, 2011

Our Kids: The American Dream in Crisis, Robert Putnam, 2016

Weapons of Mass Instruction: A Schoolteacher's Journey Through the Dark World of Compulsory Schooling, John Taylor Gatto, 2010.

The Bee Eater: Michelle Rhee Takes on the Nation's Worst School District, Richard Whitmire, 2011

Tribe of Mentors, Tim Ferris, 2017

Hillbilly Elegy: A Memoir of a Family and Culture in Crisis, J.D. Vance

The Church of Irresistible Influence: Bridge-Building Stories to Help Reach Your Community, Robert Lewis, 2002

Framework for Understanding Poverty, Ruby Payne, 2005

Toxic Charity, Robert Upton, 2012

The Present Future: Six Tough Questions for the Church, Reggie McNeal, 2009

About the Author

Brian Stroh is the Executive Pastor at Hillcrest Church. He lives with his wife Tarina and four children in Sioux Falls, SD. For more information on this book or partnering with a public school in your community, contact Brian at 605-351-2680 or email him at brianstroh@siouxfallschuch.com

Made in the USA
Lexington, KY
25 May 2018